90% OF THE GAME IS HALF MENTAL

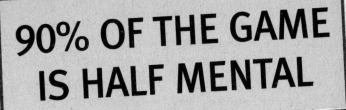

90% OF THE GAME IS HALF MENTAL

*And Other Tales from
the Edge of Baseball Fandom*

EMMA SPAN

VILLARD TRADE PAPERBACKS
NEW YORK

For my parents,
who always believed I could do it,
despite mounting evidence to the contrary

It is foolish and childish, on the face of it, to affiliate our-selves with anything so insignificant and patently contrived and commercially exploitive as a professional sports team, and the amused superiority and icy scorn that the non-fan directs at the sports nut (I know this look—I know it by heart) is understandable and almost unanswerable. Almost.

—ROGER ANGELL, *Five Seasons*

CONTENTS

INTRODUCTION:
Don Mattingly's Mustache

I worked at a used-book store in high school, and one day during my junior year, a few months before the start of the Yankees' steam-rolling 1998 season, Yogi Berra came in to do a signing for his first collection of Yogiisms. He lived in town—Montclair, New Jersey—and was sometimes spotted hanging out with a pal at the Hilltop Nissan nearby, a dealership for which he also did low-low-budget local TV ads. In fact, it was during a speech at Montclair State University that he delivered his famous line "When you come to a fork in the road, take it," advice I follow to this day.

The signing was big news at the Montclair Book Center, all hands on deck, and I was taken from my usual duties realphabetizing the romance section to work crowd control. A line formed around the block hours early, and we were instructed to make it clear to everyone that Yogi would sign his book and only his book—absolutely no baseballs, cards, body parts, or infants.

Like, I suspect, many members of my generation, at a young age I'd developed a lingering confusion over whether Yogi Berra had been named after Yogi Bear or vice versa, or if perhaps it was all just a crazy coincidence. But by age sixteen I knew exactly who Yogi was: the best catcher of all time (Johnny Bench who?), winner of ten World Series, catcher of Don Larsen's perfect game, notable quotable.

Yogi in the flesh was a bit of an anticlimax—he was a small, sturdy, gnomelike man who looked quite a bit like my grandpa Murray. He was pleasant but clearly going through a long, tiring routine, understandably on autopilot. My boss introduced me at one point, when I brought Yogi a glass of water, but I had no illusions that he'd taken any notice of me.

"Ninety percent of the game is half mental" is of course a famous Yogiism, though there's some debate as to whether he ever said those exact words. Maybe it was "Ninety percent of this game is mental and the other half is physical," or "Baseball is ninety percent mental and the other half is physical"—or maybe it was actually Phillies manager Danny Ozark who said whatever was said. I don't think it really matters, though. Someone said it, or something like it, and if it wasn't Yogi then it should have been. With old baseball stories, I'm of the "when the legend becomes fact, print the legend" school of thought.

About nine years after that book signing, I saw Yogi again, in the Legends Field locker room in Tampa, when he was a spring training advisor to the Yankees and I was a fledgling sportswriter. He looked exactly the same, and I thought about asking him if he remembered the Montclair Book Center, but once again he seemed tired after a long day, heading to change in the coaches' locker room—so I didn't make an impression on him that time, either. Maybe the third time will be the charm one day.

Like a lot of fans, I tend to track major life events by what was going on in baseball at the time, rather than the other way around—so the time between Yogi sightings stretched from the winter after the Yankees lost to Cleveland in the Division Series to the spring before the Yankees lost to Cleveland in the Division Series. But it was one of those moments that make the years feel a lot longer. Writing about sports had never so much as crossed my mind when I first handed Yogi a glass of water, and not quite a decade later, I hardly felt like the same person.

Fandom, like religion, is largely an accident of birth, a matter of geography and parenting rather than temperament, nurture more than nature. It's certainly possible to convert later in life, and plenty of people do, but it's a difficult process that forces you to question some deeply held beliefs and risks alienating family and friends.

I grew up in New Jersey in the 1980s, and because my dad became a Yankees fan, I did, too. Back then the Yankees were, so far as most kids in Jersey were concerned, Don Mattingly, and though I didn't know much about baseball back then—long before I had figured out what the deal with Yogi Bear was—I knew that Mattingly was awesome. In fact, that's just about all I remember about the Yankees in the eighties, along with an occasional flash of Winfield or Henderson. It's probably just as well that I seem to have blocked out the pitching staff.

It's hard to overestimate what a looming presence Donnie Baseball was back then. Toward the start of the 2006 season, my friend Ted, who grew up in Connecticut, sent me a text message during a Yankees game. He was watching it on an emergency-room TV, waiting to be treated for what turned out to be a collapsed lung (or 'spontaneous pneumothorax,' which would be a good name for a bad metal band), and he admitted later that it was difficult and painful to breathe. But I only found that out the next day, when his roommate called to let me know Ted had been checked into St. Vincent's—he didn't mention any of that in his text. He just wrote: "Don Mattingly shaved his mustache?!?!"

Like almost everything else, baseball fandom gets more complicated as you get older, especially when you're pulling for the Yankees, who after all have come to stand for some very unappealing things. "Rooting for the Yankees is like rooting for U.S. Steel," goes the old saying, and while the metaphor may be outdated (like rooting for Microsoft? For ExxonMobil?), the sentiment still applies. The Yankees can be tough to defend. In 2007 they outspent the Tampa Bay Devil Rays by more than $165 million; sure, the Rays' ownership were cheapskates who apparently couldn't care less about their thirty-seven fans, but that's still fairly embarrassing. So is the fracas over the public money used to fund the new Yankee Stadium, and the completely insane through-the-roof ticket prices for premium seats at the new place, which opened in the middle of a crushing recession.

I miss the days when I just had to feel bad because they spent too much money and won all the time and Steinbrenner was a dick. It was sort of like the sports fan's version of liberal guilt. Don't get me wrong—I enjoyed every one of the Yankees' World Series wins to the fullest and wouldn't trade them for anything, and given the essentially irrational nature of sports fandom itself, it's an entire level above silly to feel guilt over your team's success. That said, I can't deny that it's nice to root for the little guy, or even just for a team that the rest of the country doesn't viscerally despise. If you're a Yankees fan, you get no pity from anyone—fair enough, of course—and you spend a lot of time either making half-assed apologies for your team or telling people to fuck off, depending on your personality.

I tend to go in more for the half-assed apologizing, obviously, especially since I've long had a secret crush on the Mets. Older Yankees fans have told me this wouldn't be the case if only I could remember the 1986 World Series winners: "They were scuzzballs, these obnoxious degenerates," says my friend Mark, a teen at the time, with considerable heat more than twenty years later. "We had Mattingly and Willie Randolph, but *they* got to win. It was just so wrong."

So maybe I'd feel differently if I'd been born a few years earlier. Then again, maybe not; I've always been drawn to obnoxious degenerates. And sure, the Mets have a payroll of around $145 million as of this writing, but because Goliath is right across town in the Bronx, the Mets still get to be the little guy. Their history plays into that, too: they had such an archetypically awful beginning that even in their best seasons, at some existential level they're still the inept group who lost 120 games. Mets fans don't want to win any less than anyone else, but they're very rarely ashamed of being Mets fans . . . even if sometimes they're ashamed of the Mets.

I can't actually call myself a Mets *fan,* since I haven't been through the wringer enough with that team to earn the title—haven't suffered enough, basically. And the one year they made it to the Series once I was old enough to pay attention, they were playing the Yankees. Of course I couldn't root for them then, even though that meant trying halfheartedly to defend Roger Clemens. Go Steel!

Sports bigamy is one of the very few vices New Yorkers will not tolerate. Most social taboos—including many forms of drug use, any conceivable sex act between two consenting adults, misdemeanors, and the less violent felonies—are looked on with more leniency than trying to root for both the Mets and Yankees. On an intellectual level, I realize that loyalty to an arbitrary collection of millionaires who play a game while wearing clothes of a certain color is not really an integral moral principle or a character issue.

That said, I'm no traitor.

In between seeing Yogi Berra in my high school workplace and Yogi Berra in my adult workplace, I'd lucked into my dream job—or more accurately, into a job that had seemed so unlikely that I hadn't even bothered to dream about it—as a sports reporter for the *Village Voice*.

Covering a team professionally—even just briefly—changes things, just like everybody says it will, even if you're not actually trying to be objective. There's no cheering in the press box, as the saying goes, and you have to be as businesslike as humanly possible if you're going to be the only girl in a locker room, so when I got a sportswriting job I adapted in a hurry, rewired my brain on the fly. Almost overnight I became more detached while watching games, more invested in baseball as a whole and less in particular teams. Even after I stopped getting regular press passes, I kept a lot of that vaguely professional demeanor. I still rooted for the Yankees, and pulled for the Mets, too, if they weren't playing each other, but I was generally not so saddened after a loss or exultant after a win as I might have been a year or two before. I didn't love the game any less, but I had less emotional investment in any particular outcome. Or so I thought.

It turns out that old partisan passion is still there, even if it hibernates sometimes. I realized that in September a few years ago, during the last Yankees–Red Sox game of the season. My friend and I watched it near our Brooklyn apartments at the Lighthouse, an otherwise excellent establishment that sometimes served as an unofficial Red Sox bar. That night it was packed with extremely loud, cocky Boston fans, who completely drowned out the handful of Yankees supporters as well as my polite, professionally detached clapping. It was Clemens versus Curt Schilling, a close game; the Yankees were fighting for their playoff lives. Derek Jeter finally put them ahead by one run, but then came the ninth inning. Mariano Rivera loaded the bases, and David Ortiz stepped into the batter's box.

It was all a business. These were just men doing their jobs, and at some point it might be my job to write about them. Neither team was, objectively, morally superior to the other. The Red Sox were no better or worse than the Yankees, and neither were their fans. This had been a dramatic game and it would be interesting to see what happened next, but there was no need to get all worked up.

Except I realized suddenly that if David Ortiz got a game-winning hit off Mariano Rivera here—*Mariano Rivera*—I was going to fucking die.

Not only did I care passionately whether the Yankees won this game, it would be a personal vindication: it would mean I was right and all those loudmouthed Sox fans infesting my bar were wrong, which I wanted very badly to be the case, especially after another beer. The at-bat went on forever, and every pitch was heart-stopping. When Ortiz finally popped out, I went limp with relief, yelled, high-fived, smirked . . . and, I'm afraid, urged a few especially strident individuals to go back to Woostah where they belonged.

I got a measure of detachment back by the time I woke up the next day. But I was relieved to know that it would take more than a year or two of sportswriting to completely kill my irrational, biased, obnoxious inner fan. It might not show very often, but if you surround me with crazed Massholes, load the bases against Mariano Rivera in the ninth, and put David Ortiz at the plate? That's like getting between a mother bear and her cubs, then poking her with a sharp stick.

Something about baseball lends itself to metaphor. You can see that in the sheer number of baseball expressions that have entered everyday language: strike out, strike three, home run, on the ball, dropped the ball, off base, touch base, out of left field, get to first (or second or third) base, cover all the bases, rain check, throw a curve, screwball, batting a thousand, smash hit, on deck, on the bench, knock it out of the park, ballpark figure, bush league, play ball, play hardball, batter up, step up to the plate, take one for the team, whole new ballgame.

Beyond that, people will compare almost anything to the game. Over the years I've heard that baseball is like a poker game, that marriage is like baseball, that sex is like baseball, that baseball is like Darwinism, that baseball is like war, and—most of all—that baseball is really, when you think about it, a lot like life. I've even caught myself starting to say that once or twice myself, and the comparison is tempting. But it's just not true: baseball is nothing like life, which is why it's so great.

A lot of my friends aren't baseball fans, or sports fans of any kind, and sometimes I'm still a little surprised that I'm one myself. I was an awkward bookworm of a child, and as an adult (more or less) I'm obsessed with novels and movies and music, generally part of a culture that tends to look down on sports as the arena of jocks or meatheads—an irrational, immature devotion to a silly and unimportant game. Though baseball more than any other sport has a long-established niche for geeks like myself, as Roger Angell noted, it's often hard to defend the passion it provokes. Why does anyone care, people ask, smugly confident because they know you don't have a real answer, whether a muscled multimillionaire uses a stick to hit a small ball past other multimillionaires?

I know many people who were baffled when I tried to explain the fuss kicked up after the Mets' 2007 end-of-season collapse, when Tom Glavine, the pitcher whose terrible performance on the last day of the season cost his team the game and therefore the pennant, made a point of refusing to say that he was "devastated." "Devastated is a word used for greater things in life than a game," Glavine noted. "I was disappointed in the way I pitched." He was, obviously, completely right, 100 percent correct . . . and yet. Within the context of that game and that season and the New York Mets, it was absolutely devastating.

A few people were actually crying in the stands that day, families and friends huddled together in shock, lingering long after the game, or cursing out everyone with even a vague connection to the New York Mets. And when Glavine's words were splashed all over the media, fans were infuriated. Partly, I think, it was because no one wants to be reminded that something they've invested so much time and energy in is basically unimportant in the scheme of things—we already know that—but also because, as a direct result of all that invested communal time and energy, it actually *does* matter.

As Roger Angell continued in the above quote, "What is left out of this calculation, it seems to me, is the business of caring—caring deeply and passionately, really caring—which is a capacity or an emotion that has almost gone out of our lives. And so it seems possible that we have come to a time when it no longer matters so much what the caring is about, how frail or foolish is the object of that concern, as long as the feeling itself can be saved. Naiveté—the infantile and ignoble joy that sends a grown man or woman to dancing and shouting with joy in the middle of the night over the haphazardous flight of a distant ball—seems a small price to pay for such a gift."

90% OF THE GAME IS HALF MENTAL

CHAPTER 1

Either Why You Shouldn't Gamble or Exactly Why You Should

I wish I could tell you I spent my childhood playing stickball on the streets of Brooklyn, but in fact I grew up in a New Jersey suburb, and on the rare occasions when I was cajoled or threatened into playing a sport, I was lucky if no one wound up in need of medical attention. My lack of hand-eye coordination is legendary, and while I've made it a point to stay as far as possible from my high school since the day I graduated, I imagine people there still talk about the time I tried to play badminton.

I got into baseball the same way most people do: my dad. A native of Providence, Rhode Island, he grew up a bona fide Red Sox fan. But by the time he and my mother settled in New Jersey, after a newspaper career that had taken them to half a dozen cities, from Philadelphia to Boston to New York to Baltimore to Dallas, he'd gone rogue, following the local team wherever he happened to be. After all, in the days before satellite TV, cable, and MLB.com, your far-off hometown team was just a tiny box score in the paper. In the early 1980s my parents finally landed, settling about twenty congested miles from the Bronx, and my dad's adopted team became the Yankees.

There can't be many greater betrayals in sports fandom than ditching the Red Sox for the Yanks, particularly back then, when it looked like the Sox would never win another World Series. It seems like the kind of major life change that would require some sort of hearing or paperwork. Every few years, still not quite comprehending, I ask my father whether it wasn't hard for him to trade in his child-hood team for their most despised rivals. His answer is always the same.

"No," he'll say flatly. "The Red Sox were a nightmare — a disorder. Autumn itself was ruined because every year it was associated with the Sox's horrific collapse — every single year. And all the squawking, bitching, and cursing . . . why would I choose to bring that misery into my house?" He wants to be able look at foliage without cringing in pain, he says. "*Every year.* Dashed expectations, bitterness and depression, an incredible amount of frustration — it's a disease. I mean that, a disease. I mean . . . *every single year.* No. I wouldn't inflict that on my family."

The Mèts were actually enjoying more success than their crosstown rivals back then, in the prelude and aftermath of their 1986 World Series win. But they belonged more to Long Island than to Jersey, Shea was a nightmare drive from our house, and besides, my dad already knew the Yankees' history front to back — they were nothing if not familiar. Year by year they became more his team, and eventually mine.

Several factors combined in the early-to-mid-nineties to push my fandom to a higher level. First, Bernie Williams came up from the minors to play the outfield, and I loved him immediately — he seemed shy and had big, nerdy glasses, like me, though unlike me he would go on to become incredibly graceful, beloved by millions, and a millionaire. An introverted classical guitarist, he was the first player I imagined I could relate to on a personal level (this was long before the world was exposed to his Muzak-like jazz guitar compositions), and I paid closer attention to the games so I could keep an eye on him and offer my extremely intangible support.

Then in 1993, two things happened: the Yankees traded Roberto Kelly to the Cincinnati Reds for Paul O'Neill, and I hit puberty. O'Neill is an interesting figure, in that probably no other Yankee in the last twenty years has been quite so adored by the home crowd and simultaneously loathed by opposing fans. (It takes a truly dedicated

Yankee-hater to work up any real vitriol toward Williams or, say, the milquetoastish Scott Brosius.) O'Neill got to me because he so obviously *cared,* albeit far too much. He made that abundantly clear every time he followed an out with a furious helmet toss or vicious water-cooler beatdown. If he hit a single, he berated himself, muttering in anguish on first base, for missing the double. Blooper reels to this day show a clip of him fumbling a catch and, overwhelmed by self-disgust, kicking the ball back to the infield.

Other teams watched these petulant displays with distaste— after all, many players care just as deeply as O'Neill without feeling compelled to prove it via Gatorade dispenser destruction after every double play. And George Steinbrenner didn't help matters by nick-naming him "the Warrior," which was undeniably cheesy and eventually led to too many Pat Benatar scoreboard montages. None of this bothered me, however. You *had* to root for him, because it was painful to see anyone as abjectly miserable as O'Neill was when he failed; you feared that if he struck out in a really big spot, it might irreparably shatter his psyche.

Plus . . . he was cute. (Yes, he had what you might describe with technical accuracy as a curly mullet; it was 1993. Don't judge.)

I hate the popular image of the arrogant, entitled Yankee fan who throws an O'Neill-style fit if his team doesn't win the Series every year. But although my dad was never a terribly intense fan—he didn't live or die by the team, or mind missing a game, or explode with joy if they won or rage if they didn't—to be completely honest, he always had a slightly ruthless, Steinbrenner-esque streak in his fandom. He decided, for example, that Joe Torre was washed up way back in 2002, just one season after he'd taken the team to within an inning of an incredibly dramatic World Series Game 7 win ("Too bad you aren't old enough to remember Billy Martin—now *there* was a manager. We wouldn't even be having this conversation."). And when Bernie Williams, formerly his favorite player, began to lose his legs and bat speed, my dad immediately expressed a strong desire for management to cut him as soon as humanly possible, if not actually ship him off to the glue factory. "Unsentimental" is how he chose to describe his attitude, while often sighing (when I protested that you couldn't expect them to win *every* year, or that loyalty ought to count for something) that I was a born Mets fan, and he didn't know where he'd gone wrong.

My mother, for her part, tolerated our baseball habit but was more or less uninterested herself. She's eminently practical and sensible, my mom—I inherited many traits from her, but not those, unfortunately—and true sports fans only rarely display those qualities. There's not an obvious practical or sensible reason, after all, to devote hours every day, and maybe hundreds of dollars or more a year, to demonstrate your commitment to a sports team whose success or failure will have no measurable impact on your life. No matter how much of your heart you pour into the Yankees, after all, they will not pour their hearts into you.

My mom enjoyed going to a game every season or two, and rarely complained about our monopolizing the TV for half the year. If the Yankees won in dramatic fashion, she might make quiet approving noises on our behalf, but unlike me she wouldn't applaud, or curse an ump, or superstitiously remain in one lucky spot on the sofa to keep a rally going. Left to her own devices, she prefers to put *Law & Order* on in the background for aural wallpaper and settle in with the *Times*.

It must have been 1995 when my dad took me to my first Yankees game, because Andy Pettitte was the rookie starter. I don't know why it took us so long to get there; for whatever reason, the Yankees had been something to watch on TV instead of a live event.

Being there in person ratcheted up my passion by several orders of magnitude. I got to see my beloved Paul O'Neill in the flesh, and was relieved that he had a solid game, so the water cooler would live to see at least one more day. The Yankees beat whoever it was they were playing (for the life of me, I can't remember), and for the first time I got a taste of the infectious communal happiness that sweeps the Stadium after a good win—and when you're a geeky middle school outcast, that moment of unity, of being part of the mainstream however briefly, can be exhilarating.

In the end it was the place itself, not the game, that sucked me in. The old Yankee Stadium wasn't much to look at from the outside, at least not since its 1975 renovation: an unappealing grayish fortress, seemingly more concerned with keeping the seventies-era South Bronx at bay than with aesthetics. But I was hooked from the first moment I walked out of the concourse tunnel toward our loge seats, when the field suddenly materialized below me. The Stadium was so much bigger than I'd expected, after all those years of seeing it on our small TV, and the three-tiered crowd was buzzing; I was totally unprepared for the spectacle. It was a perfect day, too—sunny and warm, breezy, with a blue sky above the surreally green grass. Even the blocky apartment buildings and Bronx County Courthouse managed to look picturesque spread out behind the outfield.

My dad took one look at my face and grinned smugly: clearly, it was all over for me. So I asked him to show me how to keep score, and embarked on a long and fruitful obsession. We went to dozens of games over the next four years, until I went to college and he moved to upstate New York and the Stadium eventually became a place I went mostly with friends, or sometimes alone, and, for a while, for work. But I'm sure no one who loves both a father and a sports team will be surprised to learn that discussing the Yankees remained an easy and safe way for us to communicate at times when other subjects were sometimes loaded—reason enough why sports matter even though, as some people never tire of pointing out, they really shouldn't.

When I think about the hold sports have over otherwise sane people, I'm often reminded of one of my father's favorite stories from his wayward youth—not about him, but about a friend and fellow journalist, whom I'll call Sal. This happened in the late sixties or early seventies, shortly before my parents got married, and my dad was spending a lot of time at racetracks. He and Sal had been part of a loose crowd that "followed the horses" up from Florida during the season and moved north from track to track, eventually winding up in Saratoga. (He still maintains that this is the way you get to know the horses, owners, and trainers well enough to actually make reliable money at the track, and in fact, when I quit my first job shortly after college, he recommended it as a promising career path.)

So my father spent a lot of time at the track, clearly, but Sal took things to a whole other level, the usual cliché: he started losing, so he gambled more to try to get out of the hole, and soon, after a streak of massively terrible luck, he found himself heavily in debt to some scary people. Eventually his wife kicked him out and his debtors started making alarming threats.

At the nadir of this situation, in Atlantic City, Sal got an all-time great tip on a horse (whose name has, sad to say, been lost in the mists of time). It was the proverbial sure thing, can't miss, so Sal scraped up every dollar still available to him, touched everyone he'd ever met, and put it all on this horse, who was running at 19:1 odds. Then, with my father in tow, he settled in to watch the race, so nervous and hopeful he was barely coherent.

My dad says the horse got out of the gate faster than just about any he'd ever seen, "like it had been fired out of a gun," and came around the bend so far ahead of the pack that he seemed to be running alone. No one had a prayer of catching him. My father looked over at Sal, ready to congratulate him, and saw his friend's face slacken with uncomprehending shock. When my dad looked back at the track, the horse was upside down in the man-made pond in the middle of the oval, having tripped and gone flying—its legs twitching, the jockey thrown twenty feet away. Then the legs went still. The horse had drowned.

According to my father, Sal took this as a sign—how could you not?—and got his life together in a hurry. He never gambled again, slowly but steadily paid off his debts, and convinced his wife to take him back. He eventually became a successful and respected journalist, won various awards, and ended up with a comfy position at a prestigious university.

A few years later, my father said, he was hit and killed by a bus.

That story has lodged in my head because it so clearly has some kind of moral—that much is obvious—but damned if I can figure out what it is. As my father said, "This is either exactly why you shouldn't gamble or exactly why you should."

Maybe I'm reaching here, but to me it has a broader application. I may not have money riding on a baseball game, but I'm still emotionally invested in an event I have no direct control over, relying entirely on other people's luck or skill. Sports have a way of making you feel like fate's plaything—not to mention making you throw words like *fate* around in the first place. (I don't believe in fate, or in karma, omens, or portents . . . except when it comes to baseball.) And maybe that's a bad idea, but on the other hand, life is short.

Now, my father has a tendency to, let's say, amplify and adjust certain elements of a story, in defiance of pesky facts, in order to increase what he calls its "emotional truth." He doesn't do it deliberately—often he doesn't even realize he's doing it at all. He's constantly molding events into a more compelling narrative even as they're happening, and as time goes on he becomes so convinced that it happened the way he thinks it did, the way it *should* have, that he could pass a polygraph with ease. There is a great book to be written about my father's youth, but it could never, ever be fact-checked.

No doubt that was part of baseball's appeal for him. The game thrives on unfounded nostalgia, wild exaggeration, and pure bullshit, which has always been part of its charm. Ty Cobb killed a mugger in a Detroit alley! Matsuzaka throws a gyroball! Wally Pipp was replaced by Lou Gehrig because of a headache and never played in another game! These days dramatic anecdotes can often be disproved by a quick online check of the archived box score, but most fans aren't inclined to look. In fact, the Baseball Hall of Fame is located in Cooperstown because, fans were told for almost a century, that's where Abner Doubleday invented the rules during a game of "town ball" in 1839. This story turns out to be not even a little bit true. The Hall might as well have been built in some other, equally bucolic American town, but as museum curator Ted Spencer told me when I visited one snowy winter, "Try and move it." Anyway, knowing the facts doesn't make the so-called Doubleday ball one whit less awe-inspiring. It's still a good story after all.

When I was about ten, my dad convinced me that our house was haunted. We lived in a dilapidated old 1920s house, a fixer-upper that my parents never quite fixed up; the paint was peeling, the ceiling sprouting odd-colored stains, the floors sagging, the furniture shredded by time and cats. My parents were vaguely embarrassed by it and almost never invited people over, but it seemed perfectly fine to me; it had character. There was a cramped attic with slanted ceilings up an old, narrow winding staircase. And there were weird little closets tucked into the basement, which had my dad's home office on one side and a dank laundry room on the other, and otherwise was abandoned to clutter and cobwebs. It was exactly the kind of place a ghost might live. My father told me that someone had died in my room once, a long time ago. And who knows—maybe someone had.

One day my friend came over, a sweet, shy girl even geekier than myself, with huge thick glasses and a long mass of curly hair she hid behind at school. I'll call her Beth. (Beth, like many of my friends then and now, regarded baseball as something she might care to watch only if there were no footage of peeling paint available.) Her intense mother never dropped her off without a supply of bottled water, lest she be poisoned by our tap. (My own mother, eternally frugal, would buy large bottles of Poland Spring but then refill them indefinitely from the kitchen sink. Years later I tried to explain the concept of a Brita, but she was not impressed.)

My dad talked about hearing noises and voices sometimes at night, about objects mysteriously appearing and disappearing. He thought the noises were coming from the basement, he said. Beth and I tried to appear skeptical—we maintained we didn't really believe in ghosts—but we still set off to explore. There was a small room behind the laundry space, littered with old shelves, boxes, random parts, and scraps, covered in a thick layer of dust, with no light except whatever seeped over from the exposed bulb next to the washing machine. We crept farther in, whispering, and then Beth pointed and gasped because, propped on the windowsill, there was a creepy old doll, not one of mine, dust-free and carefully positioned as though it had been left there just recently. We stared at each other. Then, from somewhere overhead, came a haunting cry.

After a couple of freaked-out seconds I recognized this as my father's disguised voice and started breathing again, but by then Beth was already halfway up the stairs, screaming. It was so long ago that I can't swear there was a direct correlation, but I don't remember her coming over as often after that. My father, for his part, denied everything and continues to deny it to this day.

If baseball has one undeniably valuable social function, it's that it serves as the universal language for people trying to communicate with their fathers on otherwise tense occasions. I can hardly count the number of people I've heard talk about this, or the number of eulogies I've read that included some reference to baseball and its bonding properties. It's more often mentioned by guys, in my experience—that whole *Field of Dreams* soft-focus fantasy of playing catch with Dad, the platonic ideal of paternal relationships. But it's not limited by gender.

My dad and I were always fairly close, but we had our fights like anyone, and once in a while they were real blowouts. Nobody on earth has the ability to piss me off faster under the right circumstances, and vice versa. Perhaps our biggest and longest brawl came in my seventh-grade year—heading into the strike-shortened 1994 season, when Paul O'Neill totally would have won the batting title if he'd had more time, I will always believe—when, after a few miserable and learning-lite years at the public middle school, my dad decided I would transfer to a private school, whether I wanted to or not. (My mother may have agreed, but it was his idea and he was its spokesman.) And so I ended up very much against my will at Kent Place, an all-girls school a few towns away, affectionately known to the locals as "Cunt Palace." Our initial battle was refought annually.

We never did come to any kind of consensus about this: he still maintains that I learned much more than I had in public school and was academically well prepared for college, which is true; I maintain that the school was a soulless snakepit built on hypocrisy, conformity, and lies, which is also true. Now we mainly agree to disagree. Back then, it was fortunate that we could talk about the Yankees.

I remember my dad trying to explain to me, much as I'm sure millions of other fathers around the country tried, why a bunch of millionaires would want to go on strike. And soon after that came the start of the Yankees' golden age, with the 1996 World Series upset, the last time anyone ever referred to the team as underdogs, and the first of several times my dad told me I could skip class to go to the parade in lower Manhattan if I wanted. Now I regret passing on the offer, but at the time I was worried about missing class.

I got good grades in high school, mostly out of spite. If you do badly in class and then tell your headmistress that she's a delusional fascist with no respect for civil liberties, you won't make much of an impact—but when you say it with a good GPA, you're harder to brush off. (Though not, it turns out, *that* much harder.) In my high school yearbook I was named "Most Likely to Blow Up the School"—though in my defense, that thing went to press months before Columbine, and it was meant as a joke. Sort of.

Baseball was not popular at Kent Place—I doubt if there were ten serious fans in my entire class—and it was never really part of my persona there. I was trying to be the rebellious artistic intellectual type by then: sneaking cigarettes (and, I blush to admit, *clove cigarettes*) and gin, reading Kerouac and Kafka and H. L. Mencken. Baseball caps just don't go with this role, and never have; the game is too much a part of mainstream American culture. So I was a fan mainly in the privacy of my own home, watching the games with my dad or listening to WFAN, the sports radio station, when he drove me somewhere.

As I staggered past adolescence and got the hell out of high school, my dad and I mostly avoided major arguments. But we hit a rough patch again more recently, for a variety of reasons, as my parents were going through a divorce. My dad had mostly stopped following baseball at this point—he had moved to a farm in upstate New York and it no longer felt like a part of his life as he changed, he said, and developed new interests. So suddenly we had no buffer, no safe topic to come home to, and I was a little surprised by how much of a difference it made. We used to call each other during games when something dramatic happened—a disastrous start, or a big come-from-behind win—which may not qualify as a heart-to-heart but at least ensures regular contact. Without that, we spoke less often for a while, and less comfortably.

Any relationship worth salvaging is stronger than just baseball, of course. But that doesn't mean there weren't times when a few words about Mike Mussina might have come in awfully handy.

CHAPTER 2

The Summer of Raul Mondesi

Many of my peers seem to consider sports fandom to be largely the province of obnoxious, beer-guzzling morons. And to be fair, that might be because a number of sports fans are obnoxious, beer-guzzling morons. (Not, I feel compelled to point out, that there's anything wrong with beer guzzling per se.)

It shouldn't be hard for anyone who's attended his or her share of games or been to a few sports bars to think of examples. At Yankee Stadium, when a dozen young guys behind me break out into a shrieking chorus of "Manny is a homo!" it's easy to look around, shrink down in my seat, and wonder if this is really a group of people I want to be even indirectly associated with. There are the suited businessmen at the Stadium who blather into their cellphones all night instead of watching the game, or that obese drunk at Shea who toppled onto an old woman sitting in the section below him a few years ago and fractured her spine. These people are not a majority of fans, but they make up for that by being among the loudest.

A lot of bright people start disliking sports around middle school or high school, when jocks tend to become the enemy. It's all too easy to see professional sports as an extension of that earlier dynamic— big, dumb guys getting money, attention, and praise for no reason other than their ability to hit a small leather object with a large wooden one, while here you are, toiling for three years to translate *Beowulf* into flawless Urdu, and nobody cares.

A few years ago I randomly ran into a guy named Louis, an acquaintance from my darkest and geekiest middle school days, on 42nd Street. We got a cup of coffee and talked about our jobs, and Louis was flabbergasted. "A *sportswriter*?" he kept saying, as if I'd just told him I'd become a meth dealer. "I never would have guessed you'd be a *sports*writer."

Sports seemed to be mostly for kids who were cooler or blander or just healthier and better adjusted than me, people whose parents didn't have to beg them to stop reading *Lord of the Rings* or *The Hitchhiker's Guide to the Galaxy* and please for the love of God go outside and get some sun. Other fans in school just weren't people I had much to do with, initially because I was too much of a loser for them, and then later because I decided to cut out the middleman and preemptively alienate myself by hating 85 percent of my classmates and teachers. Except at home or at the Stadium, baseball was mostly a private passion.

That all changed in college, not coincidentally the first time since at least fifth grade that I didn't feel like a complete freak. I wasn't one of the smart kids at Yale, not by a long shot, and there were students far nerdier than I could ever dream of being. I wasn't suddenly cool, I was just average—normal—and it came as an enormous relief. I didn't have to put up such a façade. Suddenly I felt like I could be the kind of person who loves sports.

So it was that my first real experience with serious Mets fandom came in my freshman year. Maybe a week into the fall semester I met Dan, an English major and musician, a sensitive guy and a lifelong passionate Mets fan from a Connecticut town about two hours outside New York. Freshman year makes for quick friendships, and Dan and I had already bonded by the time the 1999 NLCS came around.

As you'll recall, the Mets were playing the Braves that year, and after a dramatic comeback in Game 5 they'd forced another potential elimination game, which I watched with Dan and his roommates. (One of whom would go on, years later, to become a senior speechwriter for

George W. Bush. That's not relevant to the story or anything—I just still have a hard time believing it.) It turned out to be a now-infamous four-hour epic, almost unbearably tense even if, like me, you had very little invested in the outcome.

I was casually rooting for the Mets at that point. I knew I wasn't really supposed to, but I'd disliked the Braves ever since I pegged them as smug and overconfident during the 1996 World Series. (Chipper Jones and his teammates made some comments that, looking back, were fairly innocuous, but at the time—in the heat of the first Yankees World Series of my lifetime—I interpreted them as disgustingly arrogant, and have now held this against the Braves for more than a decade.) That inclined me to pull for the Mets, and once I got sucked into the game I gradually realized I'd started to care more than I had any right to. Besides, anyone could see that if the Mets didn't pull this off, it was going to absolutely destroy Dan—he was staring at the TV with a tight, hollow, haunted sort of expression, chin cupped in his hands.

It was the eleventh inning in Atlanta and the bases were loaded with Braves when Mets pitcher Kenny Rogers, who'd been infuriatingly uneven while throwing for the Yankees three years previously, walked outfielder Andruw Jones and forced in the Braves' winning run. It was a horrific way to lose a game, let alone a playoff series. Even I was floored, and the room went silent, everyone staring at the TV in disbelief as the Braves leapt around the field, all of us apparently waiting for some miraculous twelfth inning.

Dan dealt with the disappointment in healthy fashion: he locked himself in his room for the next forty-eight hours and, while his roommates left bagels and soda from the dining hall outside his door, simulated the entire season via computer game, over and over again, until finally after dozens of tries his virtual Mets won the Series. After that he was able to drag himself back to class and resume a few social activities, but to be honest, I'm not sure he's ever been quite the same since.

Looking back, this was a pretty fair introduction to Mets fandom.

The YES Network (that's Yankees Entertainment and Sports, for the uninitiated) debuted in the spring semester of my junior year. I remember it clearly because I kept calling the cable provider to double- and triple-check that I'd be able to get it. I was fascinated from the very beginning, even though it launched several weeks before the season, with limited and therefore extremely repetitive programming. (The Paul O'Neill "Yankeeography" must have played three times a day in the early going, not that I was complaining.) Presumably because it was so new, it featured about five ads, all local and apparently on a budget similar to the one I worked with in film class, which were aired over and over again. Close to a decade later I still remember the spot for the Captain's Galley restaurant in West Haven, narrated unironically by a man with a thick pirate accent, who urged viewers to "experience the legend for yourself!"

It was heavy on the propaganda and take-no-prisoners branding, even for fans as big as me; in retrospect, I think the YES Network helped move the rest of the country's feelings toward the Yankees from mere hatred to white-hot loathing. But none of that stopped me from watching it incessantly.

My roommate, Katharine, tolerated this remarkably well for someone with virtually no interest in baseball, especially considering that when we first started living together the YES Network didn't even exist. We had and still have a lot else in common, including a shared love of movies; we were both working at the Yale Film Study Center, where we took full advantage of the free video rentals to see the kinds of classics and foreign films that had been harder to come by in high school. Katharine would often come home with a David Lynch or Truffaut DVD and find me parked in front of the television, watching the David Wells and David Cone perfect games in their entirety, back to back.

"But if it's a perfect game," she'd say, not annoyed, merely perplexed, "don't you already know exactly what happens?"

Fair point, but the novelty of an all-Yankees channel would not wear off for months, much to the detriment of my spring GPA.

The summer after the birth of the YES Network was probably the most baseball-drenched of my life up to that point, though oddly it was also the one season I followed primarily via radio. It was 2002, my second summer living in New York, this time subletting a one-bedroom apartment in Fort Greene with a fellow film major. We alternated: one month sleeping in the real bed, then one on an air mattress in the living room.

I'd known I wanted to live in the city since I was twelve or thirteen, when I'd take the bus in from Jersey and spend weekends wandering around the Village and sitting in Washington Square Park. I'm sure I looked just as pathetic as the kids I see doing that now, but I already knew back then that it didn't really matter how uncool I felt in New York, because nobody around me remotely cared one way or the other. I was sick of sticking out, and all you had to do to blend into the background on Eighth Street was not be naked and on fire.

Anyway, that summer I was supposed to be writing for a culture website. I'd gone out to Bushwick to meet the guy who ran it, and he'd given me my first assignment, a write-up of the *Star Wars* exhibit then at the Brooklyn Museum. Then, of course, the week I arrived in the city the site went under, and both it and my almost-boss vanished without a word of warning or explanation. Which meant that I was suddenly unemployed less than a year before graduation (and to add insult to injury, I'd gone to see a *Star Wars* exhibit for no reason).

In the end I did a little freelancing for a couple of local Brooklyn papers and took a job handing out flyers for Jewish singles events. I was one of those people standing on the corner, often outside Bryant Park after free movie night, and learned quickly that yelling "Jewish singles mixer this Friday" is far less effective for flyer distribution than "Free drink," which is what I started saying instead. My summer roommate was very nice, but we turned out not to have much in common—her favorite movie was *Dude, Where's My Car?* which, credit where credit's due, is a pretty gutsy choice for a film major— and we had no TV. So most nights I lay on the air mattress, turned on the radio, and listened to the Yankees.

Although it didn't end up being a hugely significant trade, I still think of those months as the Summer of Raul Mondesi. Mondesi was a perennially disappointing outfielder with a cannon of an arm, and the Yankees acquired him from Toronto in a salary dump—New York took on his $11 million annual paycheck and sent the Blue Jays a pitcher named Scott Wiggins, who went on to throw a grand total of 2.2 innings in the majors.

I don't know why some baseball moments stick with me more than others, but I remember so clearly lying on the mattress one afternoon, staring at the ceiling and listening to New York sports radio staples Mike and the Mad Dog discussing the trade. Mike Francesa was a devoted Yankees fan, but his partner Chris Russo, the Dog, as a lifelong Giants fan, hated them even more intensely. For some reason this particular trade really set him off, the spark to his powder keg.

I have warm feelings toward Mike and the Mad Dog, even if that's mostly because they were so fun to complain about. Their commentary was not often incisive or revealing; instead it was their accents and their speech patterns ("Joey in Queens, you're on the air," "The Mets fan is getting a little impatient right now," etc.) and the way news didn't really feel like news until you'd heard their reaction to it. I remember first hearing them on the car radio when my dad picked me up from middle school, and I kept listening until the pair finally split up in 2008. Given how severely they seemed to annoy each other, it's a miracle they lasted that long.

Anyway, the Yankees traded for Raul Mondesi and the Dog flipped his shit. I'm not sure why this move in particular so irked him; I suppose because it was so much money for a merely okay player, and because the Yankees at the time didn't have a burning need for another outfielder. The Dog was spluttering and yelling, which wasn't unusual for him, but with such passion and force that at least one caller expressed concerns about his health. It made for an entertaining afternoon, and it's probably one reason Mondesi stands out to me among a sea of other players who've come and gone over the years.

In the end Mondesi was only on the team for a year. He made a few great assists from the outfield, knocked out a few home runs and, per his MO, was mildly disappointing given his theoretical skills. Next season at the trade deadline the Yankees swapped him for Bret Prinz and David Dellucci. His name will hardly live in the annals of Yankee history. But he's burned into my brain, given how many hot evenings I cranked up the radio so I could hear it over the fan next to the air mattress and listen to the Yankee announcers talk about his arm, how no sane opponent would try to take the extra base against Raul.

I believe it was that summer, with too much time on my hands, that I first started imagining, once in a while, Mike and the Mad Dog's voices in my head doing a running commentary on my life. For those who haven't heard the show, picture two middle-aged Long Island–accented voices, one baritone (Mike) and one shrill (Dog); they've been together so long they could easily finish each other's sentences, and they kind of resent each other for it.

MIKE: Okay, Dog, let's talk about the job interview. I thought it was not her best.

DOG: Oh, my God, it was a disaster!

MIKE: Well, I don't know that I would say disaster. But certainly it didn't go the way the Emma fan was expecting it to go.

DOG: Oh, are you kiddin' me? Where did that come from? Her greatest weakness is her *perfectionism*? Gimme a break!

MIKE: Let's go to the phones. Joey from Queens, you're on the air.

JOEY FROM QUEENS: Hi, Mike, first-time caller longtime listener. How are you guys?

MIKE: We're good, Joey. Whaddaya got?

JOEY FROM QUEENS: Well, I think Dog's right here, and also, did you see her posture? I mean, she was slouching—it was just embarrassing.

MIKE: Yes, that's a good point, Joey. Dog, she *was* slouching. . . .

That summer was also one of the first times I ever wrote about baseball. Inspired in part by the Mondesi trade, I wrote a piece for the *Brooklyn Rail* about being a Yankees fan with a bad conscience, feeling embarrassed about rooting for such a Goliath, and then being embarrassed about being embarrassed. I'd even started rooting for the Nets as penance, only to be foiled when they suddenly got Jason Kidd and got good. I wrote, "Some people say Americans love a winner and some say Americans love an underdog, but what Americans really love are underdogs who win."

As it happened, though I didn't know it, I was writing at the end of the age of Yankees dominance. Of course they were still very good for many years, and spending even more money than before, but their string of World Series appearances broke and many listless first-round playoff losses lay ahead. The 2001 World Series turned out to have marked the end of that era.

At the same time, I was really coming into my own as a fan, caring more (and more openly), exploring the stats, going to games myself if no one else was around and sitting in the bleachers. At least the worse the Yankees did, the less I could be accused of front-running. And I was more comfortable presenting myself as a fan, because unlike my high school days, both at college and in New York City I didn't really need a "persona." I could just be myself—at the former because I genuinely felt like I more or less fit in for the first time, and in the latter because nobody gave a fuck if I fit in or not.

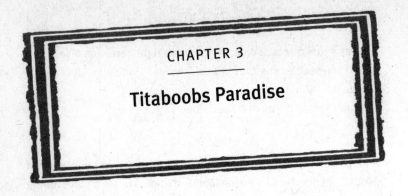

CHAPTER 3

Titaboobs Paradise

I don't know if it's a generational thing, if it's part of a broader trend, or if it's just especially acute among my acquaintances; maybe things have always been this way. But it feels like at some point, getting a good steady job just wasn't good enough anymore. You needed to get a job that played off your passions and hobbies and interests, to make what you love into your work. So you couldn't just find a steady income working at a bank, say, or managing a restaurant, and simply watch a lot of movies and go to a lot of baseball games. No, you had to *make* movies. Or write about baseball games.

I've never really had what you'd call soaring self-esteem. For most of my adolescence I figured I was an ugly, awkward loser who would never truly fit in, and I'm not sure that suspicion will ever dissipate entirely (nor am I always sure that it should). Yet despite that, I always figured that careerwise I'd do something pretty cool. Something that people would be jealous of, even. Like doing well in school, I thought, it would be my reward for being a geek.

It doesn't take much time in the real world to figure out that careers, at least the kind I wanted, are not like school: no schedule, no clear guidelines, no grading system. In class I always knew more or less what I needed to do to achieve the desired results. You didn't have to put yourself out there; you just had to keep your head down, answer the teacher's questions, hand papers in more or less on time, and make up some index cards for the final. With jobs, it's never been so straightforward.

People often lament the way the job market has changed since the good old days, when workers often stayed with a single company their entire lives. Those days are not just gone, they've been obliterated. In my first twenty-seven years, I've worked for no fewer than fifteen different employers, and I'm probably forgetting a few—in fairness, I'm counting one that only lasted a day, and two that I held for just two weekends each, but then I'm not counting any freelance writing. My very first job, at a used-book store in high school, lasted nearly three years, still a personal best.

The bookstore paid minimum wage and I started the summer after my sophomore year, when I was fifteen and thrilled to be surrounded by thousands of books so dusty and parched they made the skin of your hands dry enough to crack after a few hours of shelving. I was still a huge nerd, but I had just recently discovered—to my delighted surprise—that despite everything dozens of PSAs, assemblies, and after-school specials had led me to believe, alcohol *is,* in fact, cool.

The Montclair Book Center, like many similar stores, was like an Island of Misfit Toys in the middle of suburbia, its employees a ragtag collection of goths, nerds, cat ladies, aspiring musicians, poets, and hippies. They were not a judgmental group, so I felt vastly more comfortable there than I ever had in school. They treated me like I was normal, and it socialized me. I first tried a cigarette with my Book Center friends—didn't inhale so I wouldn't cough and embarrass myself—and out back during a lunch break I smoked up for the first time. My first Christmas there, our boss, an affable and muddled sixties refugee, gave my friend a dime bag in lieu of a bonus; I got, much to my chagrin, a scented candle. Still, things were changing, because in the simplistic world of high school, nerds just don't smoke, drink, or do drugs. Once you do, you're something else, harder to categorize. "I heard you were, like, an alcoholic!" squealed one girl in the juniors lounge after a weekend in which I'd had three beers. I was thrilled.

I would've happily stayed on at the Book Center, but I moved away for college. I took more photos at the bookstore to remember people by than I ever did at school. Of course, looking back, one of the things that made the place so pleasant was that I was young enough to have no qualms about where I ought to be working—I was in high school, so it was enough to have a job. I didn't need to worry about what I was doing with my life or why I was making only $5.75 an hour. I just needed to smoke with my coworkers and keep toddlers from chewing on the pop-up books.

Once you get to college, there's some pressure to find work that's in your field of interest or at least somewhat legitimate. But my shortest stints of employment came the summer after my freshman year of college, an idyll that all by itself accounted for four of those fifteen positions I've held. I was interning at New Line Cinema (I'm not counting internships toward the job total), unpaid, living at home in New Jersey and commuting into Manhattan, and I needed a part-time job. The first one I talked my way into was with the Princeton Review, a surprisingly lucrative position that required hours of awkward training to ensure that I'd be sufficiently perky and "on-message" while explaining to a room full of bored high schoolers how their parents' money was going to allow them to learn the tricks that would help them do better than they deserved to on the SATs. But the teaching schedule turned out to conflict with my New Line hours.

Next was a waitress position at a country club about forty-five minutes from my house, a place that wouldn't have allowed me in the front door if I weren't an employee, which grated. Still, I thought I'd give it a shot, and another waitress, a high school junior, began showing me the ropes. The dining hall was predictably full of old men in golf pants. Suddenly one of them started screaming at her: "What are you doing? You're bringing dessert *before you clear the bread plates*? What am I paying for here? What's the matter with you? Where's your supervisor?"

I followed the waitress back to the employee locker room while the manager, a smooth, unruffled woman in her twenties, soothed the golfer. "Happens all the time," said the waitress, and shrugged. The manager came into the room and turned to me, took in my standard white button-down shirt and black skirt, and said cheerfully: "I'm going to go get you a bow tie!"

She left the room, waitress in tow, and I slipped out the back door, dashed for the car, and sped away. It was not my proudest moment.

The next job was arguably my most disastrous, which is saying something. By now I was applying to essentially every ad in the *Times* classified section, back when that actually still existed on paper, and I went for an interview with a valet parking company based in nearby Bloomfield.

"Yale?" the manager asked, looking at my resume. "You're hired."

Now, I loved Yale, and I believe that I learned a lot there. One thing a Yale education has absolutely no correlation with, however, is valet parking skill. For my first assignment, I was sent with one other first-time valet parker, another college student whose name I've long since forgotten, to a massive Indian wedding reception at a restaurant an hour south, in central Jersey. There were perhaps four hundred guests there, and most of the parking was a good quarter-mile from the door. Neither one of us knew how to drive a stick shift.

This went about as smoothly as you might expect. Some guests didn't seem to be familiar with valet parking at all; dozens of stick-shift drivers who *did* know what valet parking was were left dissatisfied. Others were understandably annoyed at having to wait twenty-five minutes for their cars while we sprinted back and forth to the larger lot. We lost one man's keys, and another man's car, for the better part of an hour.

Toward the end of the night, I made the slight error of assuming a car was in reverse when it was actually in drive, which might have been fine had there not been another car a few inches in front of me . . . and had the woman who owned said car not been standing perhaps ten feet away, watching the whole thing. To this day I'll swear there was no damage, but nevertheless, there was much screaming about the police when I refused to hand over my driver's license. In the end she gained a measure of satisfaction by leaving a shrill message on my boss's answering machine, featuring what I saw as needlessly harsh language and legal threats.

I'd been wearing a new pair of black dress shoes and running nonstop all night. When the event was finally over, my fellow parker and I staggered away with around $140 each, all in singles. When I got back to my own car—really my parents' car, a lumbering old blue minivan that I had semi-ironically nicknamed Shadowfax because, again, I am a huge nerd—I noticed that the backs of my ankles were bleeding.

Much to my surprise, I wasn't immediately fired. I worked one more weekend as a valet, at an upscale wedding for perhaps two hundred guests at a deeply pretentious country club; here there were six parkers, most of whom could drive a stick and, Ferris Bueller–style, took advantage of this skill by taking the guests' Mercedes and Ferraris out for spins during the ceremony. These guys were pros and weren't inclined to let the new girl take too many cars and tips away (no matter how much she knew about the Yankees), so I only took home $20 that night. A few days later the manager told me he didn't have any other gigs available in the near future. I wondered if he had only just checked his voice mail.

I worked at the college library one year and the Film Study Center for the next three years, renting out videos to students and faculty, surrounded by free DVD rentals and TVs, still arguably the best job I have ever had. In the summers I tried and mostly failed to freelance. I got my bartending certificate, which proved thoroughly useless for landing a bartending job but was impressive at parties. I worked at an extremely upscale paper store in the West Village, handling the three or four customers a day who came in to buy vellum at $2 per sheet. I lay in my sublet or bedroom flat on my back and listened to the Yankees games on the radio, or WFAN's sports talk radio in the afternoon. I figured everything would change after I graduated.

Right out of school, aiming for an eventual screenwriting career, I got a job as an assistant at a big talent agency's New York office, about which the less said the better, except that the popular stereotypes about high-powered agents are actually far too flattering. I thought I would love being close to movies, but of course I wasn't really much closer to movies than I would have been at a drive-through window. I spent most of my days frantically scrambling to get things mailed or copied or printed, answering the seven phone lines, and lying through my teeth to whoever was on the other end, including a panoply of neurotic celebrities.

One of my bosses was a very nice British man. The other was a viciously gossipy woman who valued sample sales more than any of her clients, and was never once spotted ingesting solid food. For reasons I never did fully understand, she glared daggers at me from my very first moments in the office, and within a few weeks she was refusing to make any sort of conversation, not even a "good morning," except to gleefully point out one of my many errors. "She woke up on the wrong side of the stalactite this morning," I would snarl to my roommates when I staggered home.

Even the Yankees failed me; she was a big fan but wouldn't discuss the team with me. "How about Mussina last night?" I'd ask, and she'd ignore me, strut into her office, and call a friend to ask the exact same question. There's almost no one I can't talk baseball with, even if that's *all* we can talk about. Five months into my tenure, I was a twitchy mess, tearing up in empathy at the Zoloft ads on TV, the ones that spotlighted a sad little cartoon rock being trailed by a personal rain cloud.

In my boss's defense, I wasn't much good at the job. Looking back now, it's hard to imagine why I thought I'd excel at a position that required organizational skills above all else; I have never had any-thing resembling organizational skills. That said, working for a woman who is openly rooting for you to fuck up badly enough that she can finally fire you might fluster anyone.

When she randomly accused me of having failed to send a client's lousy script to a French producer—perhaps one of the few things I had not actually managed to mess up in my agency tenure—it was the last straw. In an emotional, heartfelt speech, voice shaking, I dis-cussed my longtime dreams of working in film, apologized for my shortcomings in the position and our inability to work together effec-tively, and painfully but with, I thought, a certain dignity, gave notice.

"Okay!" she chirped.

There followed a discouraging period of unemployment, in which I scraped a little money together by reading scripts for an eccentric, independently wealthy aspiring film producer who, as far as I could tell, never actually read any of the dozens of evaluations she paid me for. I tried a little freelance writing but was hampered by a near-pathological dread of pitching ideas and contacting editors. Finally I applied for a job at my local Barnes & Noble in Brooklyn—I needed the health insurance, and it was only a fifteen-minute walk from the apartment I shared with four college friends. Just for a few months, I figured. But over a year later, I was still there, and in fact being sent to Lead Bookseller classes.

It wasn't a bad job, which is why it was so easy to stay. Granted, nothing makes you loathe humanity in general—and Christmas in particular—like working retail, but my coworkers were on the whole terrific. There's an us-against-them feeling in any large shop, but es-pecially bookstores, which lets people of diverse backgrounds, ages, races, and personalities band together to a degree that would be downright heartwarming if so much of it weren't based on a deep shared hatred of the customer. But it was great for collecting dumb questions ("I want to learn how to speak Jewish," "Do you carry life-sized models of the Declaration of Independence?" "I'm looking for a book, I can't remember the author, but it's about how a race of interdimensional space lizards actually control what we think is the universe."). And there was the 30 percent discount. There are far worse ways to make a living.

Unfortunately, though, $9 an hour is no living in New York City, which is why when I heard from a friend about a copywriting opening "providing content for online e-tailers"—a position they had the nerve to call "film editor"—I jumped at it. I had given up for the moment on finding that dream job; at least, I thought, this involved movies. Sort of.

In practice, "providing content for online e-tailers" meant that I wrote dozens of brief blurbs about sleazy grade-Z DVD releases every week—short paragraphs that, per my well-meaning boss, "don't have to be positive but can't be negative."

There were five of us in the film department, mostly dazed, adrift onetime film majors wondering when everything had gone so wrong. Since it would have taken too long to actually watch the DVDs, our summaries were generally based on information from the distribution company or from Google, seasoned with what might kindly be termed a little creative guesswork. If you think all this sounds confusing, try explaining it at a loud party; in such situations most of us began shortening the job description to "I summarize porn."

Every now and then I was assigned a legitimate movie, each of which I synopsized with the tender care befitting a college thesis. Mostly, though, my titles were decidedly downmarket: Christian children's videos (*Incredible Creatures That Defy Evolution*), Lifetime movies, German karaoke programs, hundreds and hundreds of Bollywood titles with mangled English blurbs, ever-lower-budgeted *Girls Gone Wild* rip-offs, workout videos of all stripes, and Japanese anime porn—the least offensive of which tended to involve schoolgirls being raped by tentacled demons.

Baseball is always entertaining and enjoyable for me in its own right, but it's also, more than any other sport, a wonderful and immersive distraction. There are times—for example, when you've just finished providing a pithy description of a DVD called *Titaboobs Paradise*—when you aren't particularly eager to dwell on what's happening in your life; baseball, for a minimum of three hours a day, six months a year, gives you the opportunity to focus your thoughts elsewhere. It's much more fun to dissect Sidney Ponson's many flaws than your own. I loved weekday afternoon games, when I could huddle in my cubicle, plug in my headphones, and listen to the Yankees' radio broadcast online.

You can derive irrational but very real satisfaction from your team's accomplishments, despite the fact that aside from correctly arranging your lucky bobbleheads before the game (very important), you didn't have a thing to do with them. But the real beauty of it is that when your guys lose, it's clearly not your fault. You're bummed, and maybe kicking yourself because you thoughtlessly jinxed them with an overconfident remark, but the bottom line is, you're not responsible. Whereas the fact that, three years out of college, you're struggling to find the right words to sell a Christian kids' cartoon about a stinkbug who learns to accept his terrible smelliness through faith in the Lord (featuring the voices of Judge Reinhold and Don Knotts) . . . well, you've got no one but yourself to blame for that.

You can still find some of my literary masterpieces with a quick online search. Regarding *Hermie and Friends #6: Stanley the Stinkbug Goes to Camp,* I wrote:

> Lovable but naturally smelly Stanley the Stinkbug struggles to make friends at his new summer camp, in spite of his powerful odor, in this inspirational and warm-hearted kids' cartoon about tolerance, acceptance, and God's love.

One afternoon I spent a significant chunk of time trying to figure out how to describe a German music DVD, based on the following summary, which had been run through an automated online translator:

To the Munich Schickeria Schwabing and FANCY belong naturally!!! Once cult—always cult!! FANCY does not have a group of fans, Fancy has a Urgemeinde. These fans know for years, what they have to expect from their Idol to—TIME LOT PROPERTY AND KULTIG EXCITING ONE POPMUSIK!!! This absolute exception feature of the German Popmusik stands in the Poplexikon like a rock in the surf. Now us Fancy with its 20jaehrigen stage anniversary beglueckt!

Indeed.

Now and then, staring up at the skylight—our office, on the top floor of an old boxy building on Hudson Street near Canal, might have been pleasant had not some unknown but much-loathed lunatic decided to paint all the walls a vivid, Cheez Whiz orange—I'd wonder how long I could do this before the bitter self-loathing embedded in my work became a bit too obvious. Then I'd sigh conspicuously and turn back to my summary of the first of four volumes of *Sexy Magical Girl*: "But when a classmate is sexually assaulted by a tentacled monster, Akitoshi watches in awe as a beautiful, supernatural warrior girl rushes to the rescue and battles the perverted creature. . . ."

Things had not gone according to plan.

As an outlet, baseball was everything I could have asked for, except year-round. But the majority of my friends were relatively casual fans, if that, which meant I had a whole mess of useless information and opinion banging around in my skull with no convenient outlet. Which is why, around the 2006 All-Star break, in between anime porn blurbs, I decided with some embarrassment to start a baseball blog.

It wasn't too long ago, but even then there was more of a stigma attached to the word *blog*. It's still not one that commands respect. *Blog* sounds silly on some fundamental level, and even though by 2006 I read a dozen excellent blogs every day, it still made me think first of a young exhibitionist pouring embarrassing details of his or her personal life into cyberspace. (At least 80 percent of print media sportswriters have never lost this view, and insist on repeating the apparently endlessly rewarding insight that bloggers work out of their mother's basement, in their underwear. Only the underwear part of that is true.)

A lot of the best and smartest baseball writing I read was online, but still, it was weeks before I mentioned this new project to anyone. I called the blog Eephus Pitch, after the superslow junkball a few wily pitchers throw to cross up overeager sluggers. I wrote most of my entries at work, where I had realized months before that I wouldn't be fired unless I committed some sort of obscene felony in plain view of the CEO, and felt immediately better for having a regular vent for my writing—even if, in the beginning, I had an audience of roughly forty people, half of whom I knew personally.

One sticky afternoon in August, while working on the abovementioned *Titaboobs Paradise* ("This subtly titled program . . ."), I opened an email from Dave Blum, the newly appointed editor in chief of the *Village Voice,* and froze. My mom taught a class at Columbia's journalism school and had warned me that she had, despite my protests and to my considerable embarrassment, sent Blum a link to Eephus Pitch at the bottom of a list of recommended work by some of her students—they'd never met, but he'd asked her if she knew of any promising writers. Apparently I was going to have to forgive her: Dave had enjoyed my blog very much, he wrote. Would I be interested in covering the playoffs for the *Village Voice*?

This was perhaps the easiest question I had ever been asked.

CHAPTER 4

Pedro Pantsless and the Heisenberg Uncertainty Principle

The restricted area of Shea Stadium, which I thought of from the first as "backstage"—the long shabby hallway with field access, locker rooms, the manager's office, and so on—was reached through an unmarked set of white double doors at ground level, right near Gate C. I'd never noticed them before, and in fact couldn't find them at first, but once I did I was surprised by how exposed and accessible the entrance was. When Shea was open to the public, a security guard perched on a stool in front, but it wouldn't have been remarkably hard to sneak past, or run or shove your way in; the Shea staff was hardly the Swiss Guard. It's a thin line between the stars and their audience, but so nondescript as to be nearly invisible.

I eventually found those doors by following Ben Shpigel, the *New York Times*'s Mets beat reporter, who knew a friend of a friend on the *Times*'s soccer team and agreed to let me tag along on my first day covering the team for the *Village Voice*, just enough to keep from getting lost in Shea's mazelike back halls. (As it turned out, I would get lost in Shea's mazelike back halls on my third day instead.) I flashed the flimsy temporary credential I'd signed for at the press gate and strode past security, and suddenly there I was, through the looking glass: a long, curving, dingy gray hallway, with a wide tunnel straight ahead leading directly to home plate and framing Joe Girardi, then the Marlins' manager, as he strolled by in uniform.

This was perfect, since with all due respect to Girardi he's not the sort that inspires fan hysteria, especially back then, before he became the Yankees' manager. I did say, against my will, "That's Joe Gi-rardi," but I think I managed to sound conversational. It's a good thing I went to Shea first and not Yankee Stadium because, much as I am impressed by Keith Hernandez, my New York–trained celebrity indif-ference kicks in enough for me to maintain my cool. Had the first player I saw been Don Mattingly, I might have hyperventilated.

Getting the credential had itself been a major undertaking. The *Voice* hadn't had a sports section for years, and whoever last held the job had apparently not made many friends in PR. Most large papers have a sports editor or other staff member to handle the logistics, but I was calling on my own behalf and without a blueprint, and both the Mets and the Yankees initially turned me down. No doubt my tenta-tive, nervous, fast-talking phone persona didn't help. Even with my editor backing me up, it took many pleading phone calls and faxes over several weeks to pry a few press passes out of the Mets, and true to their image, the Yankees were even more grudging; I spent a sig-nificant portion of several days on hold while a barely comprehensi-ble recorded message from Robinson Cano assured me that my call was appreciated.

When I finally got to Shea it was late September, and I was taking a few weeks off from my DVD-summarizing job to be at the ballpark. To my eternal regret I missed seeing the team clinch their division by just one day, but the images of their wild, joyful celebration were all over TV and the papers: Jose Reyes wearing goggles to shield his eyes from the champagne, David Wright looking even squarer and more wholesome than usual when he tried to pull off a cigar, the team stay-ing on the field and exulting with their fans long after the game ended. The beat writers complained that their notebooks had gotten soaked and their cars still reeked of alcohol. Today the team was ex-pected to have a communal hangover.

I'd spent the last week in a state of steadily increasing panic: handed my dream job on a platter and out of the blue, I was terrified that I'd fuck it up. The longer I thought about it, the more I felt I had absolutely no idea what I was doing. I'd written mainly columns and reviews in the past, not many reported stories, and only a couple had involved sports, let alone talking to professional baseball players. It was the small, practical issues that I obsessed over: Where was I supposed to go when? What time should I get there? What kind of tape recorder was I supposed to have? Most of all, what the hell should I wear? This turned out to be a more loaded question than I could have imagined—my usual torn jeans and T-shirts were way too grungy, but I didn't want to stick out as too formal, either; I wanted very much to look nice but couldn't risk anything tight or low-cut for fear of seeming unprofessional.

I wasn't familiar with some of the most basic nuts and bolts of the job, and I couldn't ask the teams, since to get credentials I'd had to pretend I knew what I was doing. Instead I emailed a Yankees beat writer with a few of my painfully stupid questions (such as whether I needed to buy a recorder or whether a lot of people just stuck to notebooks). I was hoping to fit in when I got there, but looking back on that email now, even years later, I still want to crawl into a hole and die. His response, polite, yet more or less dripping with contempt ("Are you seriously asking me if . . ."), was somewhat justified, and provided me with one more thing to fret over. Perhaps now all the other writers would know I was an idiot before I even got there; usually, I thought mournfully, it takes people at least a few days to figure that out.

By the time I woke up on the morning of that first game, I was nervous enough to throw up my Cheerios.

Surprisingly—or maybe not—the restricted area of Shea wasn't in much better shape than the rest of the place. The tunnel from the locker room to the dugout boasted an ugly Astroturf-ish rug with many lumps and holes, several of those omnipresent Shea puddles that somehow managed to survive even the brightest and driest weather, and in lieu of walls mildewed hanging tarps that only partially hid the dark piles of debris on all sides. There was a tiny bathroom just before you reached the dugout, and I can recall more wel-coming stalls at Port Authority in the eighties.

I don't really want to pile on Shea, because there's a long line. I heard at least seven or eight different sportswriters express their ea-gerness to be the one pushing the plunger when demolition day fi-nally came. (They were all disappointed, as Shea was reduced to rubble slowly and in pieces.) But also because, in this age of cookie-cutter nostalgia-fest stadiums, I grudgingly admired Shea's unique ugliness. The place had character—sort of a disagreeable character, but character—and that ought to be worth something. It was a re-minder of changing times; Shea was completed less than fifty years ago, in 1964, yet it is now impossible to imagine a scenario in which anyone could look at those blueprints and think, *Good idea.*

The Mets clubhouse itself, though, was an unpretentious space, and pleasant enough. It was a long rectangle, brightly lit, slightly too small, and completely lined with locker stalls. Two big multisectional black leather sofas faced each other across the center of the room, and they might have looked impressive if not for a scattering of small, cheap fuzzy pillows in neon orange and blue, which marred the effect. There was a table in the center of the room with copies of the *Times,* the *Post,* and the *Daily News,* which most players pretended to ig-nore, as well as items to be signed for the team to sell, for charities, or just for one another's collections—photos, jerseys, boxes of balls. The lockers themselves tended to reveal less about their owners than I'd hoped, with relatively few personal items left out in plain view. Jose Reyes's appeared to be at least 60 percent full of sneakers. The room still smelled of champagne, despite reportedly heroic late-night ef-forts from the cleaning staff.

My most surprising revelation about sportswriting was that, like many other neat-sounding jobs, close to three-fourths of it consists of basically standing around. Baseball writers, thanks to the power of the otherwise largely useless Baseball Writers' Association of Amer-ica, get considerably more locker room time than writers in any other major sport: the clubhouse opens more than three hours before game time and doesn't close till forty-five minutes before the scheduled first pitch; it opens again ten minutes after the final out. In theory, this is an excellent opportunity for the press and their subjects to spend a lot of time talking and building strong, trusting, mutually beneficial relationships. In practice, most of the players spend additional time in their private lounge and training room, and so the writers stand around in clusters and gossip.

Not yet having a lot of standing-around experience to draw on, or anyone to gossip with, I used my notebook as a protective shield and wrote down every single thing I saw or heard, no matter how insignificant, which gave me something to do with my hands and somewhere safe to put my eyes. I wanted to give myself a day to acclimate before I started asking questions, so I just took in as much as I could: *Jose Reyes looks like a skinny speedster on TV, but he's a big guy in person, six feet tall . . . horse racing on TV . . . Jose Reyes, Endy Chavez, and Anderson Hernandez joke around in Spanish and crack each other up, I hate myself for taking all those years of French . . . David Wright half watches SNY's coverage of the previous night . . . everyone's talking about the crazy Dodgers game yesterday . . .*

Paul Lo Duca, coming off a string of juicy tabloid scandals involving teenage mistresses, horse racing, and divorce, nattered on excitedly to a group of reporters about how great and amazing the clinching celebration had been, until someone asked him what he'd done after leaving the stadium the night before. "Think I'm gonna tell you *that*?" he demanded, and stomped toward the training room.

I hadn't been particularly concerned about being a woman in the locker room until just a few days beforehand, when an idle Google search turned up all kinds of horror stories from the early days of female sportswriters. I knew it was bad in the beginning, but I hadn't realized that as late as 1990 reporter Lisa Olson, then at the *Boston Herald,* was subjected to hair-raising sexual harassment while covering the Patriots.

But apparently a lot has changed since 1990, and for the most part, New York athletes are used to having female writers around—a minority, but certainly a regular presence. Some days I was the only one, which made it hard not to feel self-conscious, but other times there might be three or four of us, more during the playoffs. Besides, any player who's uncomfortable with it knows better by now than to say anything rash, and anyone who tried would be set upon by a small army of PR people and hustled away for reprogramming.

This is not to say that it didn't take a little getting used to. I'm no prude, and the nudity itself didn't much bother me (although anyone who's used to being the only girl in a room of forty men, many of them naked, has led a more exciting life than I have). But sometimes there's just no good place to put your eyes, and I worried that players would think I was checking them out if I looked the wrong way at an inopportune moment. The Mets clubhouse turned out to be the easiest in this regard, because it had a pair of flat-screen TVs suspended from the ceiling, which meant I had a reliably safe place to look when everyone came out of the showers. My first day there, *The Rock* was playing; the next time it was *Saving Private Ryan*, another day *Mr. and Mrs. Smith*.

A certain segment of my friends never could understand why I wasn't taking the opportunity to ogle a little. But what they didn't seem to realize, ethical implications aside, is that if you can see the players, they see you, too—and it's hard enough to interview athletes when they don't think you've been staring at their dicks.

Of course some players are, let's say, more comfortable with their bodies than others. On my first day I'd been in the clubhouse less than an hour when Pedro Martinez walked in and started changing by his locker. I wanted to go over and talk to him—ask him a question if I could get up the nerve, or at least listen in on a group session. But I figured I would wait until he got some pants on. It seemed like the polite thing to do, probably the course of action Emily Post would suggest.

I shifted my weight from one leg to the other and fiddled with my pen; Pedro gave interviews cheerfully and joked with his teammates in Spanish. I glanced over super-briefly, so as not to get too good a look at anything, every few minutes. *Pedro* really *not in a hurry to put on his pants,* reads an exasperated scrawl in my notebook from a good twenty minutes later, *really* underlined three times. Eventually he wandered into the trainer's room, pants still nowhere in evidence.

Later I heard a Pedro story from several different reporters, none of whom had felt able to write it. Apparently during the 2005 season, two writers got into a shouting match and nearly came to blows. (For some reason this is not unheard of among male sportswriters; you can practically feel a breeze from the force with which the athletes in the vicinity roll their eyes.) They were right in each other's face, these two, almost nose to nose, when a completely nude Pedro Martinez jumped between them. He dug around in his locker and pulled out a pair of boxing gloves, which he threw down between the two reporters, and enthusiastically offered to referee a match. Sadly, they never took him up on it.

Pedro also had a Yoda mask in there somewhere, according to multiple sources, though I never got to see it in action. This is why fans love Pedro with the intensity they do; most lockers contain just piles of shoes and clothes and either Tinactin or Lamisil.

Trying to ease into things, I didn't talk to any players that first day, but congratulated myself on simply having survived three hours in the clubhouse and focused on breathing as I considered the prospect of actually, you know, *doing my job* and conducting interviews. In the end it was another reporter who calmed me down, a small, friendly, goateed man from the *Times Herald-Record* who retained a surprising amount of good humor for a longtime sportswriter. We were sitting at the same table in the fluorescent-lit cafeteria across from the press box, where the Mets were inexplicably serving alligator kebabs, and I was picking at a plate of lettuce. (There are places I might be willing to try alligator—Louisiana, a nice Cajun restaurant—but Flushing is not one of them.) Sensing what by then must have been my palpable nervous exhaustion, he smiled reassuringly.

"You'll be fine," he said. "It's not brain surgery."

This is hard to argue with. Asking a guy about pitch selection can seem terrifying from a certain angle, but from another it's as easy as anything. The next day I walked up to Tom Glavine—might as well start with the Hall of Famer, I figured, and work my way down—and ventured a fairly standard question about whether or not the Mets' vaunted team chemistry was vital to winning. Glavine, forty at the time, was known as an accessible, articulate, polite guy, and he didn't disappoint. With graying hair, thin crow's feet, and the hint of a small spare tire, he looked more like a friend's fit father than an elite professional. All he did was thoughtfully answer a question, at length, that probably didn't deserve all that much thought, but it meant a lot to me. Most sportswriters seem to have a similar soft spot for the first guy who helped them out.

It got a little bit easier every time. I was never what you'd call relaxed, but after that I talked to Billy Wagner, and Cliff Floyd, rightly famous as the best quote on the team, and Jose Reyes, who said essentially nothing but in a fun and energetic kind of way, and David Wright, who somehow manages to come across as 100 percent earnest and genuine while being incredibly careful to say the right thing.

Clubhouse chemistry is a fragile thing; the Mets that year struck me as a perfect storm of good guys having a good time, but though most of the same characters were back the next year, somehow it was never the same.

The next week I finally headed out to Yankee Stadium. The Bombers had clinched their division in Toronto a few days after the Mets wrapped up theirs, but the remaining home games were still just about sold out, and the crowd of reporters was far bigger than the one at Shea.

The Stadium's personnel and press entrance was all the way around the back if you took the subway. The Yankees had a more formal process than the one at Shea, involving huge X-ray machines, and made people without season credentials wait in a small holding pen, like stray farm animals. Once inside, it was pretty much what you'd expect: the dining area was much fancier than Shea's, for example, and my first day they served steak instead of alligator, but they also charged more than twice as much for it. The carpeting was nicer, the lighting more flattering than Shea's ghoul-toned fluorescence, and the elevator faster. Self-important security personnel went tearing down the halls on Segway Personal Transporters.

Now that each team has a brand-new building, some of these differences have been lost. Shea's flaws became part of the Mets' scrappy underdog personality, and even as they had the highest payroll in the National League, they could still claim poverty in comparison with the Yankees. That image may be a little harder to foster now that their building is all shiny and well-designed and famous for its gourmet food options.

Anyway, it's a long-standing truism (and endlessly irritating to Yankee fans) that the Yankees are a buttoned-down team, boring and businesslike. Judging from the bilingual whoops and laughter oozing out of their clubhouse showers and lounge, that may not be the case, but it was certainly true that they were less relaxed in the locker room itself. You can't blame them, though: it was a more formal space than the Mets', with miniature white façades over each locker, no televisions, and a reporter-to-player ratio that might be 5:1 or even higher at any given moment. There's certainly no shortage of press surrounding the Mets, but there wasn't quite the same feeling you got at the Stadium that any offhand remark might well end up on the back page of the *Post*. This is why Derek Jeter hasn't said anything interesting since 1997.

Even with Shea to prepare me, walking through the tunnel—under that iconic if pompous "I thank the good Lord for making me a Yankee" sign that the players tapped for luck before games—and into the Yankee Stadium dugout left me feeling very small and very lucky. Joe Torre schmoozed on the bench before games, vastly more relaxed and at ease than Mets manager Willie Randolph, who generally looked as if he'd jump at the offer of a root canal if it meant he wouldn't have to answer any more irritating questions. During batting practice I spent a lot of time just leaning on the dugout railing, taking in the view.

Don Mattingly was Torre's bench coach that year, and every time I saw him pass hurriedly through the locker room I froze to the spot and lowered my eyes like commoners used to do around royalty. He did not appear to radiate a warm divine light, somewhat to my surprise. I heard him tell another reporter who approached that he was too busy to talk, and I never did get to ask him anything. But maybe that's for the best, as I was never forced to confront the fact that he was both a mortal being and a less than riveting quote.

The first Yankee I spoke to one-on-one was Sal Fasano, the portly, light-hitting backup catcher famous for his Fu Manchu mustache and for once having a pizza delivered to his small but devout fan club (Sal's Pals) during a game while with Philadelphia. Like many of his teammates, it turned out, he was friendly and polite without actually saying all that much, but then again, they didn't know me—I'd had no time to build up relationships. Later I stood in a small group around Bernie Williams, who was soft-spoken and thoughtful but, by the time it was my turn to ask a question, gently edging his way toward the door.

A day or two later, I decided it was time to talk to Derek Jeter, and so many other reporters had the same idea that I had to get in line. The guy in front of me made small talk with Jeter about college football—Jeter is a notorious Michigan fan—and The Captain responded with easy, casual politeness. When it was my turn, I was painfully conscious of the line of impatient writers behind me, and affected by the weirdness of talking to someone I had thought of for ten years mostly as a little character who lived in my television set. In the end I managed a few questions about stolen bases and offensive production and scribbled in my notebook as Jeter once again said all the right things, about helping the team and winning games, just like he'd always done in my TV.

Like Jose Reyes, Jeter looks fairly slight on TV but is actually a big, imposing guy; you'd notice him walking down the street even if you didn't know who he was, several inches over six feet and carefully muscular, obviously an athlete. Despite his many obvious achievements—great hitter, future first-ballot Hall of Famer, media-savvy, well liked by coaches and teammates, you may have heard something about this—I never had the all-encompassing crush that many fans of all genders and sexual preferences immediately developed. (When he arrived in the majors I was fifteen and immediately determined that he was but a boy when compared to Paul O'Neill, a real man, and one who I firmly believed was attractive enough to get away with that hairstyle.)

Jeter is very likeable both on TV and in person, but he's so carefully guarded in public that I never felt I had a clear idea of his actual thoughts or personality. Since he reveals so little of himself—which I don't mean as criticism; it's understandable and probably very wise—all we hear about him, it sometimes seems, is what nightclub he was at when, and with which starlet. That is, when he's not patiently explaining for the five thousandth time that his ultimate goal is to win a championship, that he doesn't care about individual statistics and that it doesn't matter where he bats in the lineup as long as the team wins. There's nothing wrong with any of this, and yet taken together, Jeter can feel more like a press release than a human being.

In my younger days I made the mistake of reading Jeter's ghost-written and largely insipid *The Life You Imagine: Life Lessons for Achieving Your Dreams*. The premise of the book was quite simple, as summed up by this actual quote: "If you are dedicated and you work hard, all of your dreams will come true." Representative line, from the very first page: "I get to play the game I love in the most incredible city in the world. I'm young, I'm healthy, I have a terrific family, and I feel blessed that the Yankees have such great fans." Even if you absolutely adore Derek Jeter, and I did, this book will make you want to kill him with a shovel.

But the trite façade is only an intelligent reaction on his part to the overwhelming media scrutiny that faces even bench players and mop-up relievers when they come to the Yankees. The dynamic between the team and reporters reminded me, the first few days I saw it up close, of the Heisenberg Uncertainty Principle, which states that the more precisely position is determined, the less precisely momentum is known in this instant, and vice versa—that is to say, you can't study one aspect of something without inadvertently affecting another. To the extent that the Yankees are a guarded, muted team, it's exactly because of all the people who've flocked to the Stadium to tell the fans what their heroes are really like. Who's to say what the team's persona might be if dozens of us weren't camped out to study the team's persona? Reporters generally try to avoid becoming part of the story, but in Queens and even more in the Bronx, they're collectively a huge part of the team they cover.

When the playoffs finally started up, the already insane number of reporters around both teams more than doubled, and it became that much harder to get an exclusive quote or off-the-cuff reaction. Suddenly celebrities were crawling all over the place; from the dugout Spike Lee filmed the Yankees taking batting practice. I saw Paul O'Neill in the hallway once and froze like a fawn in front of a Mack truck. I shared an elevator with Luis Gonzalez and wondered what you say to the man who ripped your heart out with a bullshit ninth-inning blooper in 2001.

Whether or not you're actively trying for objectivity—writing in the first person for the *Voice,* I wasn't particularly—if you cover sports professionally for any significant period, you'll likely stop rooting for any particular team over another. It's just the nature of the work, at least if you plan to keep your dignity. My first night at Shea one reporter brought up something that had happened in 1996, which he referred to as "the last year I was a fan"; while he said it casually, in passing, it struck me as melancholy. In order to do the job right, do you have to give up a big chunk of the reason you're there in the first place?

I understand why there's no cheering in the press box—it's unprofessional, and I wouldn't do it even if it were actively encouraged. But that also means a press box is one of the least enjoyable places you can find to watch a great game: full of khaki-clad middle-aged white men and almost completely silent, at least until you get an exciting, dramatic last-minute win, at which point everyone starts cursing and scrambles to rewrite their ledes.

I was dreaming of a Subway Series—I'm always dreaming of a Subway Series—but it wasn't meant to be. The Yankees were overwhelming favorites to win the Division Series with their overpowering lineup—"Murderers' Row plus Cano," everyone was calling it—but they got crushed by the Tigers in four games.

The third of these was won for Detroit by Kenny Rogers—the same Kenny Rogers who'd folded like laundry when pitching for the Yankees in 1996, and the man who threw ball four to Andruw Jones seven years earlier as I watched in my friend Dan's dorm room. Sitting behind the mike at his postgame press conference, after completely dominating his old team, he managed to be simultaneously touching and infuriating.

"For my time being there," he said, "I don't understand New York as much as some other people, but I would think that they would appreciate the effort that people give. Not always the results that you want, but playing there for those years really made me a better pitcher, better player by far, and I think that's what New York would probably be proud of. . . . Whether I was prepared to be there or not, I gave everything I had every time out there. One of my wishes would probably be that they would appreciate that."

Nope.

The Mets fared better, and I thought they had a team-of-destiny feel as they knocked off the Los Angeles Dodgers (though since they won the third game in California, I missed yet another champagne celebration). In the Championship Series they faced the Cardinals, a mediocre team from a terrible division that made the playoffs with a winning percentage just a hair over .500.

By the time Game 7 of the NLCS rolled around, I was trying to convince myself that I was just rooting for the Mets because I wanted to get to go to a World Series for the first time. But it was more than that; I was starting to make up irrational reasons to dislike the Cardinals (e.g., Scott Spezio's ridiculous facial hair), always a sure sign of impending fandom.

The Mets had such a media overflow during the series that there were three auxiliary press areas. I was assigned to the last of these, the cafeteria, but I was damned if I was going to be at Shea for one of the biggest New York playoff games in years, with a sold-out crowd on the verge of losing its collective mind, and spend the time in a windowless room watching the game on TV. There was extra room in the auxiliary loge section, behind the plate, and no one was checking seating assignments; from there you could see the upper deck visibly shaking, which was neat but, since this was notoriously dilapidated Shea, also a bit disconcerting.

Despite the ending, this was one of the greatest games I've ever seen in person—"The Catch," right away, was all you needed to call it. It was a tense, close game throughout, started by Oliver Perez back when he was a pleasant surprise and not a wildly unpredictable mainstay. Fan favorite Endy Chavez's moment of baseball immortality came in the sixth inning, with the game tied at 1–1, when he launched himself way above the top of the left field wall (in front of a now-ironic ad for the bankrupt AIG featuring the slogan "The Strength to Be There") and flat-out stole a solid home run from the Cards' Scott Rolen; as if that weren't enough, he then hurled the ball to first and doubled off Jim Edmonds.

At this point, it was obvious to me the Mets were going to win—it was fated. How Chavez got to that ball remains a complete mystery no matter how many times I see the replay; the Mets had the nerve to list him as six feet on their website, but he most certainly is not. The entire crowd was in shock, and even reporters jumped to their feet or exclaimed, which is the sign of a true instant classic. It was the best play I've ever seen live, and not by a little.

In the end that didn't matter, though, because fate messed up. Yadier Molina, a man who had previously hit sixteen home runs in his entire worthless career, crushed one off Aaron Heilman, and the Mets fell just short of a comeback. Yes, Yadier Molina. That's why I didn't get to cover an all-time epic celebration and a World Series: *Yadier Molina*. I may never get over it.

When the game ended—when Carlos Beltran took a called third strike on a vicious curveball with the bases loaded—I went to the Mets' clubhouse first; I didn't want to go in there reeking of champagne, the smell of which was already carrying several hundred feet from the Cardinals' locker room. There were small remnants of plastic hanging from the TVs and lockers, where the clubhouse staff had prepared for another possible celebration. For a room crammed with dozens of people, it was incredibly quiet. Willie Randolph had told his team to "keep their heads up," and amidst the disappointment there was a sense of pride at what the Mets had accomplished that season. But the team still looked crushed, moved slowly, and spoke in hushed voices. I couldn't bring myself to bother Heilman, who a few days earlier had sheepishly told me that he chose "London Calling" as his entrance music because "I thought it was kind of fitting—calling the bullpen or whatever." Now he looked not so much like he was about to cry, but like he really, really wanted to.

Over on the third-base side of the tunnel, the Cardinals' locker room was swimming in champagne and beer, the floor seeping and squishy, reminiscent of a vastly out-of-hand frat party. Mookie Wilson, of all people, was grinning and gladhanding, wearing bright red; his nephew Preston was a Cardinals outfielder, but it still felt horribly wrong. I had missed the initial explosion of champagne corks, but stray Cardinals were still tossing beer around, and the air was thick with alcohol. Players were hugging, slapping each other on the back, whooping, giving stuttering, dazed, joyful quotes to damp reporters.

It's hard to watch so many people be so deliriously happy and not feel at least a little glad for them, but I did my best. As the team splashed whole cans of Budweiser all over each other and everything nearby, I stood to one side and glared silently at crappy ex-Yankee turned World Series hero Jeff Weaver.

It had started drizzling, and I'd offered another reporter a ride home, since he lived more or less on my way, just off the BQE. (I fervently hoped I wouldn't get pulled over on the way there, as the permeating stench of booze might be difficult to explain away. "It wasn't me, officer—it was David Eckstein.") But he was a serious Mets fan— his usual beat was real estate then, not sports—and still in complete shock; he wasn't ready to go. Before we left he wanted to walk out onto the field one more time.

I kept expecting security to stop us, but there was nothing to protect anymore, and no one bothered us as we stood there, taking in the empty stadium, watching drizzle settle onto the NLCS logo. Eventually I tugged at John's arm and led him gently toward the parking lot.

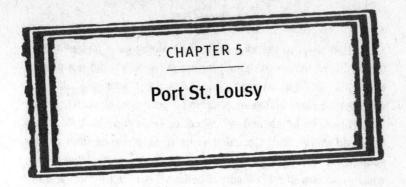

CHAPTER 5

Port St. Lousy

For serious baseball fans, spring training is the promised land, associated with all that is good and hopeful in the game, the beginning of summer, the mythic American past. For years I'd envisioned warm, sunny, lazy Florida days, relaxed banter, palm trees . . . the game in its purest, most innocent form. I'd spent the winter on a hectic tour of New York sports for the *Voice,* and this was my reward, getting back to baseball and to sunshine.

Well, it was warm, anyway, and there *were* palm trees, but on the whole things didn't go exactly the way I'd imagined. After two weeks of covering March games for the *Voice,* one spent in Port St. Lucie with the Mets and the other in Tampa with the Yankees, I found myself perched on a chair in the shiny, congested Tampa International Airport on a gray Friday morning, on standby, with a rising sense of panic, watching flight after flight to the Northeast switch from delayed to cancelled due to a major snowstorm, and correctly suspecting that if I ever did by some miracle make it back home to New York, I'd be fired by my new editor. Having just missed check-in for my 8:00 a.m. flight by three minutes, I was furious with myself, exhausted from two weeks of deep and varied awkwardness, tense, and barely able to stand up, thanks to my back, which had seized up on me without provocation during the fifth inning of a Mets–Orioles game. I missed my friends and my sort-of boyfriend and my apartment and my dog, whom I'd left with my mom, and yeah, I missed my mom, too.

I'm so used to thinking of spring training as a peaceful, sun-dappled idyll that even though for me personally it did not go that way, I still find it almost impossible to describe March baseball in any other terms. Years and years of seeing it portrayed as such in books and articles, on blogs, and in languid, relaxed television broadcasts have had their effect. I couldn't seem to stop myself from writing about it accordingly while I was there; I wanted to protect that image, which is so powerful I still sort of believe it—there's a "spring training" in my head that's separate from the spring training I actually saw.

Now, sportswriters should never, ever complain about their jobs. Few things drive passionate baseball fans crazier, and many of them aren't that enamored of sportswriters to begin with. Disgruntled readers and viewers, irritated by repetitive or insipid coverage, or sometimes just by perceived negativity toward their team, will often talk about "the media" as if they were a single entity, a malevolent cabal that consciously decided to make Mets manager Willie Randolph's job security an issue, or to overrate Derek Jeter's defensive skill, or to cover Alex Rodriguez's infidelities. It can seem that way because there's no denying that the media coverage influences the way we see a team and a season, and because groupthink can sometimes take over in sportswriting like it can in almost any job. But there's no agreement, no industrywide plan, no conspiracy, just a varied group of people trying to do their jobs, some harder than others.

To be fair to spring training, my main problem really had little to do with the games or the institution itself; it was that when I left I was pretty sure that I was about to be fired. I tried to convince myself that I was just being pessimistic and neurotic, per usual—I've often been convinced I was about to be fired, and usually it was all in my head—but for once I was right. Getting to tell colleagues and friends "I told you so" has rarely been less satisfying.

A few weeks after the 2006 NLCS, the *Voice* had hired me full-time, and I spent that winter scrambling from one iconic sports venue to the next—a few weeks in the epic disaster zone that was Isiah Thomas's Knicks; a few weeks with the Rangers; Christmas Eve at the

Giants game and New Year's with the Jets. It was a terrific and fascinating experience, though I was often out of my element. I've always liked and followed basketball, but I don't know its intricacies as confidently or intuitively as I know baseball's, and as for hockey and football, let's just say I was learning on the job. No one wants to be that person, and especially not that *woman,* asking ignorant questions in the press conference; I was weighing every word that came out of my mouth, trying not to make any mistakes. For all the stress, though, I loved my job, the first ever that felt like it could actually be a career, and not just a paycheck.

It was an eye-opening immersion into the culture of New York's massive sports media. More than any other American city, with the possible exception of Boston, New York's sportswriters are loud, influential, and inarguably part of the story. Teams and players distrust reporters, but it's a symbiotic relationship, however dysfunctional.

The *Voice* had recently been sold to a national chain of alternative weeklies and was something of a mess. There had been months and months of turmoil, waves of firings and layoffs, nasty press coverage, leaks from pissed-off longtime employees and from the strident new owners, and thickly flying unconfirmed rumors. Dave Blum, the editor in chief who'd given me my shot (also the man I'll be naming my firstborn child after, even if it's a girl), had hardly been given a chance to put his mark on the paper yet. When I started there full-time, my cubicle was the only one occupied at the end of a deserted row. The other desks had never even been cleaned out: people had left, or perhaps been escorted out, without bothering to pack up, and the little enclosures were full of furniture, books, notes, files, even a few half-full coffee mugs. It looked like everyone had suddenly fled for their lives, and every time I walked by I thought of Pompeii.

The *Voice*'s owners fired Dave on a Friday, for no good reason that I could see, about twelve hours before my flight left for Florida. A new editor—the *Voice*'s fourth acting EIC in less than two years—might well want to bring in his own people, and I was Dave's hire, so I knew

I could be in trouble. But there was nothing I could do except get on my plane. Besides, there was a silver lining:

"If they can't find me," I told my coworkers, "they can't fire me."

Once in Florida I picked up my rental car, a boxy nightmare called a Dodge Caliber—a model I had never heard of before and have never seen since, which managed to combine mediocre gas mileage with limited space and huge blind spots. The radio brought my first taste of culture shock: alternating Christian stations and country music all the way up the dial.

Tradition Field, spring home of the Mets and not to be confused with the Yankees' Legends Field, is a charming, open park that I fell for the second I realized there was a thatched tiki bar in the left-field stands. (I'm easy.) It seats about seven thousand, with low fences and not much in the immediate vicinity besides grass and parking lots, giving the place a calm, flat, rural vibe.

It does have the misfortune, however, of being in Port St. Lucie, which does not actually contain a port of any kind, and which has long been known to beat writers as "Port St. Lousy." There may well be more to the town besides highways and strip malls, but I didn't get to see it; it mainly reminded me of stretches of New Jersey near where I grew up, only with better weather and a few palm trees. There's not much to do at night beyond bowling and arcade games, which is good for keeping the players out of trouble but bad for the overall sanity of anyone staying there more than a few weeks. There's apparently a proper beach within easy driving distance, but I didn't have time to look for it and in fact never even glimpsed it, though I did once catch a whiff of sea breeze from the Walmart parking lot.

Tampa, where the Yankees spend spring training, is certainly a step above Port St. Lucie, but I found it didn't have much to offer me person-ally, given my strained financial situation and lack of interest in strip clubs. But the baseball venue itself is as pleasant as you'd expect. The Yankees' spring training facility, now Steinbrenner Field, is really nothing like the old Stadium—low to the ground, clean, new, surrounded by grassy sun-drenched parking lots rather than by the South Bronx. But there are unmistakable Yankee touches, from the mini–Monument Park to the highly Steinbrennerian man-made swan pond near the gate. It's less formal than the Stadium—security a bit less uptight, smaller distances between the players and the press and the fans. The corridors outside the locker room, leading back to the practice fields and weight room and batting cages, are still your basic dank hallways, though—interrupted only by the occasional office door and the press cafeteria, which bore an eerie resemblance to the one in my middle school.

For a while in college I considered majoring in anthropology, and I never regretted the decision not to until I spent significant time in New York press boxes. It would take a trained professional to really do justice to the customs, alliances, cliques, feuds, and taboos of the tribe. And if you *were* doing a study of the sports media, there could be no better setting than spring training: uprooted from their daily lives, families, and civilization as we know it, set free in the wilds of Florida with limited expense accounts, the scene took on an unnerving *Lord of the Flies* quality.

The press dining room at the old Yankee Stadium impersonated a restaurant—carpeting, polished wooden tables and chairs and, though it never managed to lose the basement feel, relatively flattering lighting—but the eating area at Legends Field has no such pretensions: it's a cafeteria plain and simple, with linoleum-style floor, fluorescent lights, plastic furniture, and mushy home fries. Trying to figure out where to sit, clutching a tray of gray food, I found it impossible not to feel like I was back in seventh grade: Which table did I belong at? Sometimes there was a friendly face for me to sit next to, other times not. Once I sat down with a few of the bigger-name writers, when I didn't see an open seat anywhere else, and realized my mistake when they all ignored me—still a nerd trying unsuccessfully to interact normally with the popular kids.

Adding to my discomfort was the fact that for my first week in Florida, I happened to be the only woman covering the Mets. There'd been days when that was true at Shea as well, or in the Rangers or Knicks locker room, and it always made me self-conscious. This was true even though no one really made an issue of it (I'd like to assume that anybody who didn't like me was just being sexist but, sadly, that seems like a bit of a stretch). It had more to do with my personality than anything else, since I'm prone to self-consciousness in interview situations even when I'm not the only woman in a large room full of half-dressed men. And the locker room dynamic between players and the media can be inherently awkward, regardless of gender.

One coach did insist on telling me, every time he walked by, to smile, because I was so much prettier when I smiled. He wasn't trying to be hostile, I think—in fact, probably he meant to be friendly, though I'd imagine by the sixth or seventh time we had this exchange it was pretty clear that I wasn't enjoying it much.

"How come you never tell *them* that?" I'd ask, gesturing toward a cluster of balding forty-year-old men, or "Why don't you ever say that to Murray Chass?"

I spent a week at Port St. Lucie before heading to Tampa, and during that time the only women I spoke to face-to-face were a Wendy's employee, a liquor store clerk, and a couple of hotel receptionists. More than half of my friends are men, and I generally feel perfectly comfortable hanging out with a group of guys, but by the time I sped away from Tradition Field for the last time I wanted nothing more than to get a pedicure and watch *Pretty in Pink*. When I finally reached Tampa I spent my first few hours in the Yankee clubhouse clinging to *Star-Ledger* reporter Lisa Kennelly like a drowning man to a life preserver.

To reiterate: sportswriters should never complain about their jobs. When you get paid to watch games, you basically need to shut the hell up about the annoyances of travel, or the dulling of pleasure in the games, or the awkwardness of the locker room. It's a dream job for thousands if not millions of people—it was mine.

So I didn't mention many of my qualms in my *Voice* columns. Just like everyone else, I was going to uphold the myth of the beautiful, relaxed, pastoral spring training I'd expected to find. And for all my whining, there really were some great, relaxed, intimate moments, the kind that were much more difficult to come by in the more intense and scrutinized New York City atmosphere.

One day I spotted Yankee middle relievers Scott Proctor, Brian Bruney, and Kyle Farnsworth gathered around the fenced-in artificial pond next to the park before a game, feeding bread to a swan. (Bruney later told me it was "sweet," and apparently lonely, having recently lost its mate.) That was going to go in my story for sure. Then there was the scene in Port St. Lucie when rehabbing Mets pitcher Juan Padilla, sprawled on the clubhouse floor, attempted to dissipate the daily boredom by whipping through one card trick after another in front of a semi-impressed audience that included Ramon Castro, Carloses Delgado and Beltran, and Korean-born pitcher Chan Ho Park (who jokingly offered to translate Padilla's rapid-fire Spanish for the assembled reporters, many of whom had witnessed this exact scene several times already). This was the kind of faux behind-closed-doors stuff (reporters aren't generally allowed behind the *real* closed doors) that I'd always enjoyed reading myself, even if it wasn't exactly groundbreaking.

And once I got used to being in the locker room, or as used to it as it was possible to get in a few weeks, I asked a few more questions and started to feel a bit more confident. I talked about photography for a couple of minutes with Aaron Sele, who had a state-of-the-art digital SLR in his locker. I checked in with Julio Franco a few times until I was pretty sure he might actually have begun to vaguely recognize me. I watched Shawn Green, in the throes of a horrendous slump, get batting tips from half the clubhouse, Franco and Carlos Delgado and Carlos Beltran and anyone else who wandered by. In Tampa I saw Don Mattingly play first base, an acid-flashback moment, during a simulated game for Andy Pettitte, while Jeter and A-Rod ribbed the old Cap about his rusty fielding.

Very few of the players were ever mean or outright obnoxious. Mostly, especially the bigger names, they were just on autopilot, answering similar questions again and again, every day. As a rule of thumb, the less famous and talented the player, the better the interview—maybe because their egos hadn't yet been inflated by money or adoration but mostly, I think, just because they weren't as sick of the questions. You get a relatively unknown twenty-one-year-old kid up from AA ball, he's usually excited to be interviewed by the New York media. Presumably the bloom will be off the rose a bit by the time he's talked to fifteen people a day for ten years. Perhaps the nicest person I encountered on either team was Wil Nieves, a sunny, engaging backup catcher who was well regarded for his game calling but, unfortunately, a completely useless hitter (.164/.190/.230 in his Yankees career). He was that rare player who would not just respond nicely to a question but actually stop to ask how you were doing as he walked by in the clubhouse and seem to really want to know (and if that does not seem striking to you, you have not spent much time covering professional sports). In fact, his Baseball-Reference.com page is as of this writing sponsored by the above-mentioned Lisa Kennelly, who eventually left the *Star-Ledger* to take a job in Seattle, and it reads: "The nicest backup catcher in the world."

Some of the most abrasive personalities I ran into in the locker room didn't belong to the players. No one wants to be portrayed in the papers as a jerk, so there's some incentive for athletes to be polite—but when it comes to reporters, nobody's watching the watchmen. It's a competitive atmosphere, obviously: the guys from the *Post* are always trying to scoop the guys from the *News,* and vice versa; everyone's looking for a fresh or different story, and those aren't easy to find or protect. Sportswriters are colleagues and often good friends, but they're not really on the same team.

In the Yankees clubhouse one morning, a few hours before what-ever the game was that day—it's so unimportant in spring training that you sometimes hear players asking each other which team they're facing less than an hour before game time—I was standing around awkwardly, as usual, waiting for the players I wanted to inter-view to emerge from the lounge or trainer's room and stand by their lockers. I had yet to master this art—I didn't want to stand *right* in front of my target's locker, because it seemed a little stalkerish and, if the guy came out in just a towel, inconsiderate. (I never did ditch my "wait for the interview subject to put on pants before approaching him" rule, though it cost me a number of quotes.) On the other hand, if you stand too far away, another reporter is almost guaranteed to swoop in and get to the guy first. Then you can wait your turn, but there's no telling how long it will be or whether the player will stick around afterward for your questions. It's an art, and the best sports reporters seem to have a sixth sense for it—the placement and timing that will ensure the best chance of direct eye contact with the least nudity.

Anyway, this particular morning I was waiting around like a very timid bird of prey when Jason Giambi walked over to his locker, across the room from me. He was one of the players I most wanted to talk to, and I hadn't had the chance so far—Giambi was at his locker fairly often (unlike, say, Alex Rodriguez) but is such a good quote that he's much in demand. So I made a beeline for him, along with a TV reporter—a friendly guy who, like me, was fairly new to his job. We were both beaten to the scene by *New York Post* columnist George King, who is respected for his years of knowledge and excellent sources more than for his cuddly personality. I retreated to the middle of the room and resumed fiddling with my pen, scanning the room for targets.

It was only two or three minutes later that King started raising his voice.

"Are you *eavesdropping*?" He had turned away from Jason Gi-ambi (who suddenly appeared fascinated by his shoelaces) and was shouting at the TV reporter, who looked around in an attempt to give off a "who, me?" vibe.

"Are you *fucking eavesdropping* on my *fucking private conversation*?" King was screaming now, getting red in the face, and the entire locker room went dead silent: players, writers, trainers, everyone stopped to listen.

"No," said the TV reporter nervously, "I wasn't eavesdropping. I mean, I was just waiting to talk to him—"

"You were fucking eavesdropping! Get the fuck out of here!"

"If I heard anything, I wasn't going to *use* it or anything—I was just—"

"Get the fuck out of here!"

The TV reporter caved, turning and making the long and silent walk to the exit, all the way across the room, escorted by a flustered media relations staffer. A few seconds after he left, everyone raised their eyebrows and resumed their business, quietly at first. King shook his head and returned to his talk with Giambi as if nothing had happened. I stood there drowning in relief that I'd backed far enough away.

I should say here that there are also many extremely nice, smart, friendly, and sane reporters covering each team. Lots of people were perfectly approachable, willing to help out when I found myself at a loss as to the proper protocol or the schedule, and full of great anecdotes and funny, cutting one-liners—protracted sportswriting experience tends to foster a dry and cynical sense of humor, which I appreciate. These people are, however, by and large less interesting to write about, which is why they're getting short shrift here.

Besides the competition aspect, beat writers struggle with the dozens of miscellaneous writers and reporters who come into the locker room for a few days or weeks, write what they want, and then leave the regular team writers to deal with any potential fallout. People like me, in other words—though, sad to say, I never got the chance to dig up any real dirt, and if I ever had written anything mildly controversial, it would have been read by only the sixteen or so *Village Voice* readers who actually cared about sports.

I met John Koblin, a *New York Observer* writer, during the 2006 playoffs at Shea. He was a huge Mets fan and occasionally convinced his editors to let him do a sports story. He made the trip to Port St. Lucie and Tampa a week or two before I did. While covering the Yankees he did something that would seem reasonable to many news reporters but was met with stunned disdain in the press box: he wrote about a conversation he'd overheard.

Now, to be clear, John wasn't wiretapping or anything. He was just standing near Brian Cashman and a group that included ex-GMs Gene Michael and Bob Watson while they talked shop. They weren't talking *to him,* but he also wasn't hiding his presence, and they never said anything was off the record. They just either didn't notice John there or, more likely, assumed he'd follow the usual sportswriter code of conduct and not write about anything negative seen or heard outside the parameters of an interview. For whatever reason, the group talked freely in front of him, and John got it all down.

Their conversation shifted from light clubhouse gossip—how tough-guy third-base coach Larry Bowa rubs himself with baby oil after every shower—to Watson's playing days, when he would steal opponents' signals and whistle them to Reggie Jackson.

Cashman said that he was trying to convince former catcher Mike Stanley to come out of retirement and coach—in part because of his uncanny ability to steal signals.

"You know who would never steal signals is Jeter," he added admiringly. "He doesn't want any extra information. He wants to go up there and take on a pitcher one-on-one."

"Like basketball," said Acorsi.

"Yeah, and you know who is exactly the opposite? A-Rod," Cashman continued. . . . Cashman speculated that

A-Rod "always has too much information. He thinks he knows an entire pitcher's profile, and then he'll take educated guesses." When he gets into slumps, Cashman said, it's often because of an information overload. It's what makes Rodriguez occasionally "look so bad."

It's good stuff—hardly BALCO-level shocking but considerably more honest, or at least uncensored, than Cashman can generally allow himself to be with reporters. When it was published, the Yankees were horrified; so were many of the beat writers.

This is a tricky issue. Frankly, I don't think I would have used that material, though it would have been tempting (and certainly I would have listened in). Whether Cashman had any reasonable expectation of privacy in that situation or not, he clearly didn't intend to be quoted, and I'd have been uncomfortable doing so—I never did write about the few private conversations I overheard, though I figured anything shouted to a teammate across a media-infested locker room was fair game. Still, a majority of the non-sports reporters and editors I've talked to had no problem with John's *Observer* article.

Much of the press box, though, was still grumbling about it when I arrived at Legends Field almost two weeks later. They had a right to be annoyed: this kind of thing makes it that much harder to get their subjects to relax around them, harder to get to know players and officials, harder to convince anyone to trust them. And while John might or might not drop by once or twice more during the year—if he was allowed back at all after this—the beat writers are there every day dealing with the repercussions. But I still thought it was telling that some writers were absolutely flabbergasted that someone had violated the usual sports beat protocol. They saw it as a tragic lack of understanding of the unwritten rules.

"They have to stop letting *these people* in," declared one prominent beat writer to his pal, with a glare—"these people" here referring not to any ethnic or socioeconomic group but to writers for weekly or monthly publications.

I was standing at the dugout railing one day before the 2006 playoffs kicked off, just a few weeks into my new job, early for batting practice but too embarrassed to turn around and go back into the clubhouse so soon after leaving. So I just stared out at the field and mostly empty stands and took in the sights while I waited for the players to take the field and stretch, and the rest of the reporters to trickle out.

The first people out, several minutes before anyone else, were a catcher and the pitching coach, who plopped down in the dugout, maybe six feet from where I stood, and began an in-depth conversation—"How about your boy last night?"—in which the catcher complained about a young relief pitcher's poor attitude; the guy had repeatedly shaken him off the night before, apparently refusing to listen or execute the game plan.

There's no way they could have missed seeing me there—no one else was in the dugout—and I was obviously a reporter, a girl with a credential holding a notebook and a tape recorder. Maybe they didn't think I could hear them. More likely, though, they assumed—even though at that point I'd only been in the locker room a few times before—that I wouldn't write what I was hearing.

And they were right. Even though at this point surely no one would care (this isn't exactly the Valerie Plame case here), I find I still don't want to put names to this story.

Anyway, the regular writers' problems with the *Observer* piece were valid, yet I'm not totally comfortable with a scenario in which reporters find themselves self-policing, essentially doing some of the team's PR work for them. None of these writers, from what I saw, would deliberately lie or misquote anyone, but they do censor themselves. They don't really have a choice. The hope, for them and for the readers, is that by omitting certain unflattering truths or unguarded remarks in the short run, they'll get more access, find a greater number of trusting sources, and be better able to have their finger on the pulse of the team in the future. I didn't stick around long enough for that to pay off for me, so my discretion was largely wasted, but in general this is a well-intentioned and practical method for navigating some tricky ethical issues. I'm just not sure it always works the way it's supposed to.

The simultaneous highlight and lowlight of my spring training adventure was a daylong road trip to Fort Myers for a Mets–Red Sox game. The Red Sox locker room opened at eight, and Fort Myers is on the other side of the peninsula from Port St. Lucie, so I got up at four-fifteen to make sure I'd get there in time. I wanted to talk to Craig Breslow, then a minor league pitcher who'd been one year ahead of me in college, and to Curt Schilling, who had a long-standing reputation as an excellent quote/blowhard (depending on whom you asked) and who had just started his own blog—one of the first star athletes to do so, and not via PR flack, either. So I was eager to ask him about that; if many of the regular writers weren't crazy about feature writers, that was nothing compared to the fountains of bile provoked by the mere mention of the word *blogger*. It was still pitch-black out when I left and, for the first couple of hours, ridiculously foggy; at one point I nearly drove off the road into what I imagined was alligator-infested swampland.

At Fort Myers, I pleaded my way past the reluctant security guard—I was on the list, but the Sox camp was then overrun with more than a hundred members of the Japanese media, thanks to a frenzy over Boston's newly acquired Japanese ace Daisuke Matsuzaka—and into the clubhouse. Many of the marquee players were keeping to the relative sanity of the private back rooms or, like David Ortiz, sitting at a table and therefore off-limits (the couches and tables in locker rooms being magical media no-fly zones). I spotted Curt Schilling, though, plopped on a stool in front of his locker.

"Hi, excuse me," I began, my standard opener. "Do you have a minute?"

"No," said Schilling, making eye contact for a second, then returning to his newspaper.

I nodded, backed away, and then watched from the middle of the room as he sat reading the paper for the next half hour.

In Schilling's defense, at this point I noticed that my pen had been leaking ink all over my hands for at least several minutes. Between that, general exhaustion, nerves, and my rumpled suitcase clothes, I was pretty much a literal ink-stained wretch. And of course even Curt Schilling must get tired of attention sometimes, and there's nothing so wrong with a player not wanting to talk once in a while, or needing a little time to himself. But I would have been more inclined to be understanding about it had I not gotten up in the middle of the night and driven across an entire state. At least it was a notch up from Michael Strahan, who had once looked at me like I was roadkill in the locker room of Giants Stadium and said flatly, "I don't talk on Wednesdays."

The beauty of spring training games is their lack of urgency, but this same quality means it's tricky to write much about the games themselves. This particular day, Terry Francona was holding forth with reporters in the Sox dugout, several of whom brought up that day's Mets starter, Chan Ho Park:

FRANCONA (suddenly puzzled): Wait. Who's pitching today?
REPORTER: Chan Ho.
FRANCONA (more puzzled): Really? . . . Who does Ohka
pitch for?
REPORTER: Toronto.
FRANCONA: Oh—that's tomorrow then.

The game itself was fun in that lazy spring training way, since I got to watch Tim Wakefield work on his knuckleball, and though Boston won 9–5, it didn't actually matter. The sun was starting to get low when I left for Port St. Lucie, but it was still above the horizon when I was stopped for speeding (apparently, those "speed limit enforced by aircraft" signs aren't total bullshit after all) and handed a $150 ticket. When I stopped at a gas station near Lake Okeechobee a little later, a thirty-something guy tried to follow me into my car, pleading with me to drive him and his mother to the nearby racetrack. I wasn't too many miles further down the highway when my lower back started to tighten up, only to lock completely during a game the next day, leaving me hobbling around Tradition Field like an eighty-year-old, barely able to sit or drive.

I realize I'm over the sportswriter complaint limit here. No doubt it still beat rotting in a cubicle summarizing anime porn. But it wasn't the greatest forty-eight-hour stretch of my life, either.

The day of my return to New York (I kept trying not to say "civilization" for fear of sounding like an obnoxious NYC-centric snob, even though that's pretty much what I am), I woke up an hour late, at 6:00 a.m., in the La Quinta motel on Tampa's glamorous West Gandy Boulevard, where the immediate neighbors included an auto-body repair lot, a pawn shop, a check-cashing place, and a Hooters. After weeks of improbably managing to lurch out of bed at dawn or earlier on little sleep, my luck, or at least my cellphone alarm, had finally failed.

By the time I grabbed my bags off the vaguely sticky carpet, checked at least seven times to make sure I had my notebooks, laptop, and digital recorder, took a wrong turn off West Columbus Drive, and dropped off my hunchbacked little rental car, I was three minutes too late to check in, according to a stony Continental Airlines employee who was unmoved by my best big, damp puppy eyes and wavering voice. All I wanted to do was get home, and now, possibly stuck in godforsaken central Florida for the weekend with no hotel, no car, and a credit card dangerously close to its limit, I trudged over to the terminal and waited for the lucky standby names to be called on what looked like the last flight to brave the nasty ice storm in the Northeast. I moped over how much I missed the city, my dog, my friends, my bed, healthy food, and regular interaction with other women.

The only silver lining was that I was pretty sure I couldn't get canned if I never got back. Still, I was anxious to meet and attempt to impress the new *Voice* editor, Tony Ortega, with whom I'd had only one brief telephone conversation earlier in the week, and to whom I was supposed to turn in my big preseason baseball cover story on Wednesday.

It would be my first career cover, and my chance to show the new guy what I could do, so it needed to be great. The spring games by themselves had not been the stuff of baseball legend—weeks of pleasant warm-ups that had somehow morphed into a massive annual media event, lots of fun for snowbirding fans but hard on a reporter looking for a unique story, since the outcomes and stats could hardly be less meaningful. Every other sentence I wrote seemed to begin "It's only spring training, but . . . ," yet a jaded throng, myself now included, swarmed to exhaustively chronicle every hiccup.

Around eleven, still fidgety as I waited to see if I'd be able to squeeze onto the next flight, I took out my paperback copy of *Red Smith on Baseball*; I'd dog-eared so many pages to mark lines and paragraphs I wanted to remember that the thing could barely close.

"You don't see people reading Red Smith very often these days," said the fit middle-aged man next to me, accurately, although your odds are probably better in Tampa in March than in most places. He turned out to be a sports agent, crisscrossing Florida to see his various clients, and he represented several players on both New York teams. We introduced ourselves and talked a little shop—how his clients were doing, how their injuries were healing, what each team's chances were. He agreed that the Yankees were looking formidable, and as we talked, I began to perk up.

The mark of career satisfaction, I think, is actually being happy when someone asks you what you do for a living. That year, for the first time, I was thrilled by the question. Admittedly, sportswriter isn't exactly up there with firefighter or oncologist or structural engineer on the useful-to-society scale, but I was still proud to say it. Seven months in, I suspected that even though the day-to-day routine of the job seemed to wear people down, that pride wouldn't fade quickly.

Moments after the agent and I exchanged business cards—another element of the job I was embarrassingly pleased by; I'd always wanted a card—my name was called for standby. I practically sprinted onto the plane, and once it was safely, blissfully in the air, I looked over my notes from the last two weeks, piecing the story together in my head. I didn't have any breathtaking scoops, but there were some decent scenes, and even a few quotes that didn't involve the phrase "I just want to help the team." Thank God for Jason Giambi. As far as I was concerned at that moment, he could inject steroids into his eyeballs if he wanted, so long as he was good for some lively quotes.

Moises Alou and Shawn Green had been eloquent. Jose Reyes had been affable but unenlightening, which was problematic, since he was clearly the most exciting player on either team at the time; ditto David Wright, an incredibly good-natured guy who wouldn't say anything controversial if you pulled his fingernails out one by one. Over at the Yankees' camp, I'd worked up a thesis about how the team's at-long-last return to supporting its farm system was good for morale. Andy Pettitte had given me good material and confirmed my theory. Minor leaguer Kevin Thompson had concurred. Johnny Damon and Giambi had played along in their role as fun clubhouse guys working diligently to loosen up the Yankees' stuffy atmosphere. Young outfielder Melky Cabrera, coming off a solid and unexpected year and speaking through a bilingual young clubhouse attendant, had thanked God and Joe Torre roughly an equal number of times. I had five days to write the piece, and so, assuming the plane didn't go down in a cataclysmic fireball, everything might actually be all right.

We landed uneventfully on a deiced runway a few hours later, and I have never been so thrilled to see either an ice storm or Newark.

Three days later, I walked toward my editor's office, reminding myself to be confident, to sit up straight, and not to talk too fast (futile; I am forever reminding myself of this and always, always forgetting it within forty seconds). We'd shaken hands the day before, we'd spoken briefly on the phone while I was in Florida, and I'd pitched some ideas in the staff meeting along with everyone else, but this would be our first real conversation.

Ortega saw me coming and rose with a smile. "Follow me," he said, striding away from his desk and toward the HR office.

Much like a horse on its way into the glue factory, I sniffed the air and knew full well I shouldn't walk through that door, but I went anyway; civilization does nothing but frustrate our healthy fight-or-flight responses. If I'd followed my deepest instincts, I would have kicked him in the shin and run, and probably been happier for it.

His exact words are something of a blur, and I just remember fragments, including "I've reviewed your previous work," "not what we want for the *Voice,*" and, repeatedly, "a matter of taste"—reason enough, under the paper's union contract, to fire anyone at any time. When I asked for more specific reasons—any reasons—he simply repeated himself.

"It's a matter of taste."

"But I just wonder what it was that—"

"It's a matter of taste."

"Yeah, I understand that. But it would help if I knew—"

"It's a matter of taste. Mihlee will help you with the paperwork." He walked out in the middle of my next sentence.

And so I packed up my notebooks, threw out a giant box of business cards, scooped the Bernie Williams bobblehead off my desk, grabbed a few friends and some Kleenex, and made a beeline to the nearest bar.

My time in the press box had been eye-opening, often a pleasure but equally often disillusioning, though not always in the ways I'd expected. I had worried that, like some sportswriters, I'd stop being a fan and lose my passion for the game. I never got to that point, but I wasn't sure how I was going to go back to yelling and cheering, either, or even if I should. There was a kind of detachment that was new, for better or worse.

My first game back at the Stadium as a civilian, I felt a twinge, walking down from the subway platform, that I wasn't heading to the right—to the far side of the building and the staff/player/media entrance, where I'd flash a credential and blow past security while ordinary fans, those poor saps, looked on from behind the barriers.

(Never mind that on the occasions when I'd been credentialed at the Stadium, I typically had to wait fifteen or twenty minutes for the staff to find my name on a list, call up to confirm, stare at me skeptically, ask repeatedly for identification, then finally and with great reluctance have someone walk down with the handwritten stick-on one-game credential that would get me in for the day, though of course only after several guards pawed through my purse and laptop bag; it was the *idea* of the credential that I missed.) This was not a feeling I was proud of, an unseemly desire to feel special. And now here I was heading for the bleacher entrance with scalped tickets, unhappy at reverting, like Henry Hill at the end of *Goodfellas,* to being an anonymous schmuck.

At the same time, it felt a little strange to be at Yankee Stadium for Opening Day without a Yankees shirt on. In previous years I usually went with my old standby, "O'Neill 21," though I also had an equally outdated "Soriano 12" and a "Martinez 24" at home. It had been my habit since that first Stadium game, part of my routine of rooting, and even if I was coming from work, usually I'd slip a T-shirt on in the office bathroom on my way out the door. It was a sign to whomever I sat next to on the subway or at the game or stood in front of in the concession line that I was one of them, and I felt a little naked without it.

I'd been debating the issue all morning. I was a fan again, but suddenly slightly embarrassed by my fandom. When you spend time with sportswriters, there's a natural dynamic of Us, Them, and Them— reporters, athletes, fans—that's hard to avoid.

Besides, what if I ran into one of the beat writers? What would they think if they saw me in a Yankees shirt? How insanely unprofessional would that look? Sitting in the bleachers, which at the old Yankee Stadium had their own separate entrance and were located as far as possible from the press box, the odds of this happening were more or less zero, but the idea had lodged in my head. I wore a plain T-shirt under my sweatshirt. To this day I'll wear a Yankees shirt around my neighborhood, to the gym or the store, or to sleep, but not up to the Stadium.

Unless they're playing the Red Sox, anyway.

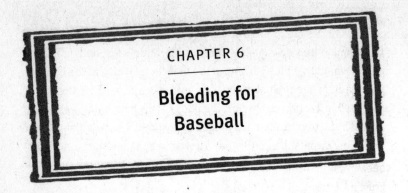

CHAPTER 6

Bleeding for Baseball

One of the most-cited baseball quotes ever is attributed to Walt Whitman and like so much of baseball's early history, is possibly apocryphal. "I see great things in baseball," Whitman (may very well have) said. "It will take our people out-of-doors, fill them with oxygen, give them a larger physical stoicism, tend to relieve us from being a nervous, dyspeptic set, repair those losses and be a blessing to us."

I don't know if I'd go quite that far—fans watching their team in a taut playoff game are nothing if not nervous and dyspeptic, and as to repairing our losses, there's only so much baseball can do. But I don't think it's a stretch to say that it can serve some kind of larger social purpose.

Part of what I've come to appreciate about being a fan is the ability to connect with complete strangers, people with whom I might share nothing except that we both happened to be born to parents who root for the Yankees. That rare chance is why I love taking the subway up to the Stadium, watching as the train gradually fills with people in Yankees paraphernalia—hats, jackets, shirts, jerseys, backpacks, baby outfits—and with conversation about the team as it moves north through Manhattan. Almost every Yankees fan I know feels that they're in the process of getting priced out, a trend that started after the first few Joe Torre–era championships and went into hyperdrive with the opening of the new Stadium. Yet, at least for now, there's still a dramatic mix of types and demographics at the games—

no more so than in New York generally but, for once, all on more or less the same page. Which is why the Bronx-bound 4 train can lead to one of those scarce moments of urban camaraderie and bonding, where people have the same temporary openness to each other that you otherwise get only during, say, a massive snowstorm.

I still remember fondly one trip to the Stadium in what must have been 2004 or 2005. Kevin Brown was scheduled to pitch—an aging, grumpy, expensive former All-Star and, like most Yankee pitching acquisitions of this era, a complete disaster in New York. I believe he was coming back from an intestinal parasite at the time, but it may have been the strained back, or the hand he broke punching the clubhouse wall.

I was standing toward the end of a subway car near two thirty-something white guys in suits, heading to the game straight from work. The thinner one turned to his friend and asked, loudly so as to be heard over the train noise, "So, how long do you think Brown will go tonight?"

The train had fallen quiet just then, and his voice carried. Half the subway car turned around—Hispanic teenagers, old Jews, blacks, whites, Asians, couples, families—and chimed in:

"Three."

"Five." (This guy was jeered.)

"Two!"

"Three and two-thirds."

Not many things in this world can unite such a group of New Yorkers, but a passionate shared contempt of overpriced, underperforming free-agent pitchers is one of them. No matter our differences, we all suffered the same agonies watching Kyle Farnsworth pitch in a close game.

I don't want to romanticize the old Stadium, which certainly had its share of assholes and dingbats. (Mets fans will argue it had many more than its share.) Still, it was sometimes capable of providing those odd slices of community, and was surely one of the few places where an investment banker, a cluster of Bronx teens, a Taiwanese tourist, a family from Westchester, and a couple of retired Brooklyn firefighters could conceivably have a lot to talk about.

Like many fans, I worry that ticket prices are shifting too much toward the banker, Westchester, and tourist side of the equation—and these days maybe not even the i-bankers can swing it. It's too soon to say, as of this writing, how much the new Stadium will change the composition of the crowd, particularly in combination with the current recession. The truth is it's been a long time since good seats in the Bronx were affordable for the average family.

A few years ago I sat right in front of a sharp-faced white guy in his late twenties who spent the better part of the third inning yelling at the flustered young mother next to him because, he claimed, her toddler son had spilled mustard on the man's $200 pants. The boy apologized when prompted, but that did nothing to keep the guy from bellowing at the two of them throughout several at-bats, until eventually he either tired himself out or noticed the fixed death-glares from everyone else in our section. It's hard to imagine this kind of douchebag loudly berating a small child over designer pants fifteen or twenty years ago at the Stadium without getting beaten up, and while I'm a nonviolent person and believe this is a change for the better, still, I couldn't help wishing someone would at least *threaten* to beat him up.

Though Shea Stadium was very different from the Yankees' much-hyped "Cathedral," the same camaraderie could take hold there, maybe even more so. Even the most spirited defenses of Shea tended to start out with disclaimers like "No matter what anybody says . . ." or "Despite its reputation . . ." When it went it was the fifth-oldest ballpark in the country, after Fenway, Wrigley Field, the former Yankee Stadium, and, by just one year, Dodger Stadium. It was ungainly, poorly designed, falling apart, inefficient in its concessions, bathrooms, and sightlines.

But anyone who's been following a team for a long time will be attached to its ballpark, regardless of its flaws. I have some warm memories there myself: Shea is the site of my first professional sportswriting experience, first player interview, first time in a press box or dugout, and the most exciting playoff game I've ever witnessed in person—Endy Chavez's catch in Game 7 of the 2006 NLCS. In fact, it's technically where I saw my first-ever baseball game, though it hardly counts because I was so young. (A friend of my dad's got us tickets to a day game, but at six or so years old I wasn't ready to enjoy the experience. All I can remember from that day are the orange seats and the hot sun.) So I was sad to see the place go this year, and I can only imagine how much more intense that feeling must have been for serious lifelong fans. But while Citi Field might not prompt reminiscences of slow summer games with your dad or the '86 World Series, on the plus side it will not constantly be compared to "a DMV without the atmosphere," either.

What I liked about Shea, though, is that precisely because of all the many things wrong with it, there was really only one reason to go. It wasn't much of a tourist attraction; it wasn't a particularly big draw for businessmen or women trying to impress colleagues and clients; it wasn't an architectural treasure or a hip place to be seen. And that's what worked about it, perversely: you went to Shea only if you loved the Mets.

One of my most unexpected friends is a sixtyish retired teacher named Linda, someone I almost certainly never would have had the occasion to speak to if it weren't for the Mets and Shea. In a move that I still have trouble classifying—it's either an admirable venture or a personal low—I went to Shea on a muggy, overcast July afternoon, while the team was on the West Coast, to donate a pint of blood in exchange for free Mets tickets.

The Mets have run this promotion with the New York Blood Center for a number of years. Shea, like a school building on a holiday, was oddly quiet on off days, deserted and strange—a functional building without a function. A few team employees ambled around, and a small stream of donors trickled in. The blood drive itself took place down a hall from the press box, in and around the Diamond Club Restaurant, which was slightly reminiscent of a mall food court even at the best of times, and was now thick with folding chairs and nurses and cots.

I noticed Linda, my fellow blood donor, before we actually met. We walked into Shea at the same time, through the big glass doors between Gates C and D, usually reserved for office employees and business visitors—an unaccustomed entrance for both fans and reporters, so I felt like a trespasser. Linda had no such qualms. We signed in at a desk, received wristbands, then waited for the elevator up to the loge level, an elevator I knew from painful personal experience to be among the slowest in all of New York.

Linda, an athletic woman with short brown hair and practical clothes, began plucking with irritation at her neon-orange wristband. "It's too tight," she muttered. "Why would they make it so tight?" She strode back to the desk and instructed the young man there in no uncertain terms to give her a looser one, which he meekly did.

"Can't even put on a wristband right. I mean, how hard is it," she demanded of no one in particular as she returned to the elevator, "to put on a wristband so it doesn't *cut off your circulation*? I mean, really."

Linda was born into an Italian family in Yonkers, giving her an authoritative New York accent that decades in the suburbs, before she moved to her current apartment on the Upper West Side, had done very little to blunt. On top of that, she spent most of her career teaching middle school, and it shows. Linda is not the sort of person you lightly decide to argue with.

After separately filling out the elaborate paperwork pledging that we had not recently been prostitutes, gay men, or intravenous drug users, nor had sex with prostitutes, gay men, or intravenous drug users, Linda and I found ourselves lying down with needles in our arms on parallel cots. It was late afternoon and the blood drive was winding down; the woman who went over my paperwork informed me that, sadly, I had just missed seeing Mr. Met, or as she put it, "that guy with the huge head." The few scattered donors left were outnumbered now by the blood center staff. I had a view of the empty field just to my left, looking forlorn with the players on the other side of the country.

Linda and I finally struck up a conversation when we made a simultaneous request for our nurse to turn the nearest Diamond Club TV to the SNY network. (She couldn't find it right away, and for a few moments we all thought the TV just couldn't get SNY. Sure, it would be crazy for a team's restaurant and club not to receive its own channel, but if this could happen anywhere, it could happen at Shea.) Watching the highlights of the previous night's loss, we began by discussing the Mets' bullpen problems, a conversation we would continue for the better part of two years.

Linda, it was immediately clear, knew her stuff. She talked batting order, bullpen management, and, in what would come to be something of a mantra, Willie Randolph's unwillingness to use the squeeze bunt. It was a surreal conversation to be having with a tube slowly draining blood from your arm, but also a welcome distraction.

Even more than most sports fans, I've found, Mets fans express love for their team primarily through complaints. It's often funny but occasionally brutal, and maybe easy to miss the love at times if you're a player on the other end of it, but it fits in well with the long-standing New York tradition of complaining forcefully and at length about just about everything, at which Linda was a master. She went smoothly from Jose Reyes's inability to be selective enough at the plate to her nurse's slowness to get her a cup of water, the blood center's limited selection of food to replenish our blood sugar, and the staff's apparent intent to rush us out so that they could close down. She wasn't wrong about any of it, only much more vocal than I tend to be in these situations. (I'm shy about criticizing service, and Mr. Met would have had to yank out my intravenous tube and drink my blood before I'd have gotten up the nerve to say anything.)

We picked up our free tickets afterward, surprisingly noncrappy seats: upper deck, but not too far out past third base, and not too high up, for an August game against the Padres. I usually get light-headed after giving blood no matter how many granola bars and cups of apple juice I'm plied with afterward, so I took the walk back to the subway deliberately slowly, because if there's one place you don't want to pass out it's the 7 train, and Linda and I chatted on the long slow ride back to the city.

Now, I knew, with a growing anxiety, that at some point I was going to have to come out as a longtime Yankees fan. Linda is fond of saying that she actually has some respect for the Yankees and it's their arrogant jerk fans that she loathes, and she was warming to her theme. By this point, having been writing professionally for close on a year, I felt I could get away with saying that I was more or less a detached observer of both teams, that I wanted them both to do well but wasn't *precisely* a fan of either anymore. Still, I wasn't far enough removed from fandom to really denounce it, and I couldn't lie by omission and represent myself as a Mets fan, however much genuine goodwill I had toward the team.

In the end Linda took my halting confession of having grown up rooting for Satan's spawn surprisingly well. I think she understood that none of us can help how we're raised, and besides, it would be hard to present clearer proof of goodwill toward the Mets than losing a pint of blood to the cause. In any case, as the 7 train neared Times Square, we agreed to meet a few weeks later in our adjacent free seats, at what I'd come to think of as the "blood game."

Not every Yankees fan hates the Mets, but every Mets fan loathes the Yankees with a fierce, bottomless passion, honed and fed over entire lifetimes. It's tempting for Yankees fans to shrug all that off as jealousy over the Yankees' success, but Mets fans inherited this abhorrence of everything the Bombers represent from previous generations of Dodgers and Giants fans, and I doubt it would lessen significantly even if the Mets won every World Series over the next three decades while the Yankees finished last thirty years straight. (Of course, the vast majority of Mets fans have some Yankees fans in their pool of family and friends; the hatred is more abstract than applied, fortunately for all concerned.) The rivalry is no longer about championship rings, if it ever was, but about bedrock values and morality. "I don't see how you can be an ethical human being and root for the Yankees," a friend told me once, not really joking.

The jerk in $200 pants I encountered at the old Stadium fits the image most of the baseball-loving country has of Yankee fans: entitled, arrogant, demanding. Needless to say, I don't agree—but more to the point, is there really any kind of prototypical Yankees fan, or a true Mets fan archetype? We're talking about millions of people, all living in the same metropolitan area. Can any group that large really have clear defining characteristics? Are the two crowds really significantly different?

Logically, I think it's pretty obvious the answer here is no. Too many people support each team—they just aren't going to all be that similar, like how the hundreds of millions of Scorpios in the world won't all find that next Tuesday is a good day to start a new relationship, whatever their horoscopes might say. And Yankee and Mets fans, like it or not, are likely to have a lot more in common with each other than with Rangers or Brewers season ticket holders.

And yet . . . I can't quite completely write off the possibility that if you are a serious fan and spend years and years emotionally invested in a team and dealing with the results, it might leave a bit of a mark on your psyche. It's nothing so simple as "Yankees fans are arrogant," but is it really so farfetched that people who spent their formative years watching Mariano Rivera close out games might have slightly different expectations of life than people who were watching Armando Benitez? (If so, that would give Mets fans a bit of an advantage, as life on the whole is much more like a Benitez appearance, in my experience.) And though both teams themselves have changed drastically since their inceptions, with entirely different owners, personnel, players, and stadiums, they each have certain threads running through their histories, if you're looking for them.

For example, the Yankees have been in the news in recent years for the shady shenanigans surrounding the financing of their new Stadium, a process that apparently involved a significant amount of public money and not much transparency. I expect New Yorkers, myself included, would be more outraged about all this if we could actually understand the complicated financial rules involved. But this is hardly the first time in the Steinbrenner era that the Yankees cut some legal corners—Steinbrenner himself was temporarily banned from baseball after hiring a private detective to dig up dirt on Dave Winfield, and he was actually convicted, before that, of making illegal contributions to the Nixon campaign and obstruction of justice. And the Boss and current team leadership have nothing on the original owners. Like your grandfather used to complain: these modern guys playing today, they just don't stack up to the old greats.

In 1903, American League president Ban Johnson was in such a rush to get a team into New York that he announced the move before securing either a ballpark or owners. This was a tactical error, since the National League Giants and Brooklyn Superbas (the proto-Dodgers) weren't keen on the competition and had enough contacts, friends, and paid-off officials in Tammany Hall to make Johnson's life difficult. Every time the AL tried to buy land for a ballpark, the Giants' friendly politicians acted swiftly to either turn the proposed site into a protected city park or, failing that, put a road through the middle of it. Eventually Johnson had to purchase a plot in secret from the New York Institute for the Blind, a feat he pulled off only by bribing his very own brace of officials.

That's why the Yankees' first owners were a shadowy group of *Gangs of New York*–style corrupt political insiders that boasted Frank Farrell and William "Big Bill" Devery as its most prominent members, two gentlemen whose criminal adventures make George Steinbrenner's Nixon contributions look like donations to the Jimmy Fund. Farrell, the "Pool Hall King of New York," was the head of New York's biggest illegal gambling syndicate; as one historian put it, he "owned 250 pool halls and almost as many politicians." He had a saloon at Sixth Avenue and Thirtieth, where he became fast friends with Devery, a police captain at the station down the street.

Known throughout the city for his talent for graft and astonishing ability to wriggle out of well-deserved criminal charges, Big Bill (who at over six feet and 350 pounds was not ironically nicknamed) went on to become New York City's chief of police. (Later he would repay the NYPD by stealing the interlocking NY design it had commissioned for a posthumous medal of honor—awarded to an officer shot and killed in the line of duty—for use as his baseball team's logo.) Devery was at various points in his career charged with neglect of duty, failure to proceed against "disorderly houses" in his district, extortion, and blackmail, but he was never convicted; little wonder, since he was also known for a cheerful willingness to bribe juries. As the *Times* put it rather delicately in its 1919 obituary, "Mr. Devery had a most picturesque and stormy career." Today's unethical baseball team dealings, while sordid, are bush league in comparison.

Furthermore, in the *plus ça change* department, when the soon-to-be-Yankees got off to a rough start in 1903, frustrated outfielder Wee Willie Keeler told reporters: "With such an aggregation of stars as we have, we ought to do much better."

Meanwhile, the Mets have fielded plenty of excellent teams since 1962 and won the World Series twice, but they never have quite shaken off the lovable loser label that their first season burned indelibly into fans' brains. (Granted, as the years go on, the crowd at Shea has seemed less and less willing to give them the "lovable" part of the equation when things go badly.) It wasn't just the 120 losses, and it's not just the inevitable comparisons to the Yankees that force and/or allow the Mets to be perpetual underdogs no matter how good or rich they become; the team, even when playing at its peak, has a tendency toward organizational ineptitude that vacillates, from era to era, between charming and infuriating.

One of the constants in Mets history, from the very beginning, is their oddly endearing penchant for ham-fisted marketing decisions—a true gift, honed throughout the years, for well-intentioned yet disastrous promotional efforts. This resurfaced most recently in 2006, otherwise a generally excellent season at Shea, when the Mets announced in mid-April that they'd embraced a new team song—or as the press release termed it, a "fan celebration song." It was performed by someone named Aghi, and debuted online in mid-April.

"We are thrilled and flattered that TJS and Breakthru picked up on the excitement of the season and recorded this upbeat, high-energy song," said Dave Howard, executive VP of business operations, as quoted in the release. "We hope that fans catch on to 'Our Team. Our Time.' as a rallying cry for the start of a thrilling season at Shea."

This hope was destined to go unfulfilled, as across the tri-state area, the country, and the globe, thousands of Mets fans clicked and listened with dawning horror. The lyrics were half rapped over an odd, mid-eighties-style hip-hop beat, and the overall impression was of someone who was trying desperately to appeal to young people but had not met anyone under thirty for a quarter of a century:

New York Mets—Our team! Our time!
New York Mets—Our team! Our time!
Our team! Our time!

We get the hits (hits!)
We score the runs (runs!)
We shut you down (down!)
We're number one (one, one, one!)

Pedro Martinez will strike you out
Billy Wagner coming through
He's throwing heat no doubt

David Wright, Jose Reyes making sure you're not safe
Just in case, Carlos Delgado, he's at first base

A quick survey of fan responses at the time, from various blogs and message boards:

- "I am embarrassed."
- "Good God!"
- "Who could have possibly thought this was a good idea?"
- " 'David Wright, Jose Reyes making sure you're not safe' is not the most creative nor the most intimidating trash talk I've heard. Forget the Mets . . . this could set *hip-hop* back a couple of decades."
- "How did the song accurately predict all the Mets' 2006 roster moves when it was so clearly written in 1988?"
- "Something tells me we're not the target market for this."
- "I think the target market for this song is deaf people."
- "At the risk of piling on, it blows."

This came just six short years after the Mets embraced the Baha Men's execrable "Who Let the Dogs Out?" as an unofficial rallying cry during the 2000 season, until it ultimately became "Who Let the Mets Out?" capped by a live performance at Shea before Game 4 of the Subway Series. The 2006 Mets were good enough not to need any mortifying tunes to inspire the crowd, and in the end the new theme sparked "fan celebration" only when it was quickly buried. In 2007 the team wisely did not release any new compositions, but they did plaster Shea with a new slogan, "Your Season Has Come," which flashed across the scoreboard frequently—even in the last days of September, when said season was collapsing in sharp, painful fragments around them.

A failed theme song is a harmless affair in the grand scheme of things, but this was just the most recent in a long line of bungled public relations efforts. Back in the team's earliest years, before the hy-drocephalic Mr. Met became a beloved fixture, they had Homer. Homer was a cute little beagle that appeared in commercials and at-tended the home games. Trained by the man famous for working with Lassie, he was at first supposed to sit in the dugout with the team, but manager Casey Stengel (who had apparently spent enough years with the Yankees to feel that this was beneath his dignity) disliked Homer intensely from the very start and nipped this idea in the bud.

The brainchild of then-sponsor Rheingold beer, Homer, according to a copywriter who worked on the Mets account at the time and wrote to Roger Angell about it, was trained to run around the bases in celebration after a home run and then "slide" into home. Everything went fine during the dry runs, but when the Mets finally hit one out during a home game and released their hound, Homer touched first, then second—and then careened cheerfully into the outfield, where he romped for several minutes while at least three staffers and a good chunk of the Mets defense vainly attempted to corral him. He was, so the story goes, sent back to California on the next available flight.

This was at least sort of a cute idea, if cheesy; less explicable is Mettle, the little-remembered mule who had an ill-fated stint as the Mets' mascot in the late seventies. Mettle was kept in a pen beyond Shea's right-field fence during games, near the bullpen, and accord-ing to the accounts of some traumatized eyewitnesses was some-times forced to wear a straw hat. Before and after games he lived in an increasingly odorous stall underneath the stands.

This debacle can be blamed on Lorinda de Roulet, the markedly less impressive daughter of original Mets owner and beloved society woman Joan Payson. De Roulet received the mule as a present from a neighbor on Long Island—why anyone would want to give their neighbor a mule is a question not answered by contemporary ac-counts of the incident—and decided to put it to work as an atten-dance draw in 1979, in lieu, I guess, of acquiring good players.

This was not a good time for the Mets, who had still not recovered from the horribly botched trade that sent Tom Seaver to Cincinnati in

1977. And so, in an effort to drum up publicity and excitement, the team ran a contest to name their new mule. The author of the winning pun, one Dolores Mapps of Mercerville, New Jersey, was announced before a game on July 8 (also Lee Mazzilli Poster Day) before a highly unimpressed Shea Stadium. She won a spring training weekend in Florida, and the Mets promptly lost to the Padres, 11–3. Quipped Parton Keese, covering the game for the *New York Times:* "Unfortunately, the Mets showed their Mettle before the game, not during it."

Adding insult to injury, Lorinda's daughter Bebe occasionally had poor Mettle pull her around the warning track in a small cart before the start of games. This display inexplicably failed to impress the crowd or inspire the players, and Mettle was eventually retired.

However many promotional misfires they've had in the past, I'm a fan of the blood-for-tickets event, especially with prices the way they are—even though it is a little unsettling to think that Mr. Met wants your plasma.

Linda showed up at the blood game with Betty, one of her closest friends and her college roommate back in 1962, when they both became fans of the brand-new, historically terrible team. Betty lives out on Long Island now, where she and her husband are also huge supporters of the independent Long Island Ducks, and neither she nor Linda attends all that many games these days—but they talk on the phone frequently, often while watching the Mets on TV. Betty is quieter and less prone to outbursts than Linda, but they are a team, complementing each other.

Linda and Betty agreed, as we watched the Mets struggle and lose a close one, on some of the team's problems: Why on earth was Carlos Delgado (a train wreck at that point in the season) still batting as high as fifth? Why did Reyes always seem to be trying to hit home runs and popping up? And why, for God's sake, was Guillermo Mota still trusted in a close game? If they didn't exactly see the team's September collapse coming, they certainly picked up on the warning signs.

"Carlos Delgado should be strung up by his balls," grumbled Linda after a particularly ungainly at-bat ruined an attempted Mets comeback in the ninth inning (though she later amended this to a mere "dropped in the batting order").

That carefully honed teacher's tone came in handy when a fidgety and oblivious boy in front of us, perhaps ten or eleven, kept standing up and blocking our view.

"*Excuse me,* young man," thundered Linda with unmistakable authority. "Stay in your seat." The boy did so instantly and for the rest of the game. I raised my eyebrows. "The trick is to tell, not to ask," she explained.

Linda also has a low tolerance for the ear-shattering Shea noise—the taped celebrities yelling "Let's go Mets," the songs of widely varying quality, the sound effects—which make it so difficult to carry on a conversation at the game. It truly is hard to understand the thinking behind this (the Yankees do the same thing); the Mets seem to take it as a given that no one wants to be able to think or talk to their neighbors, and while I sound cranky and old complaining about this, I honestly don't know anyone who enjoys hearing "Everybody clap your hands!" at a volume so thunderous it makes one's teeth rattle. Besides, the chants of "Jose, Jose, Jose, Jose," as set to the "Olé" melody, were vastly more fun when they were spontaneous and sincere, instead of canned and prompted.

"I don't go to games anymore because of this—so loud you can't even hear yourself think," Linda told me on more than one occasion—though it should be noted that on each of those occasions we were, in fact, at a game. "It's enough to make you lose your hearing. Think what this would do to your ears if you came here all the time!" She was planning to write a letter to Keith Hernandez about it. (Many Mets fans have an unshakeable belief in the inherent ability of Keith Hernandez to fix just about anything.)

She'd been going on this vein for several innings when she spotted a young man in khakis with a Mets identification card hanging on a lanyard around his neck—some kind of low-level team employee, patrolling the stands. Linda was out of her seat and had him button-holed near the concourse entrance within seconds. She launched into a litany on the earsplitting noise, the unsafe decibel levels, and the disrespect and condescension of it all, while the young man, who after all was not in any way responsible for any of this, could only nod nervously, unable to get a word in edgewise.

Linda finished with a flourish: "And furthermore, I've been a fan of this team *for more than forty years*," she wound up, "and I *do not need to be told when to clap*!"

I don't doubt that the fans around us would have stood and cheered, if only they'd been able to hear her over the music.

CHAPTER 7

Frankie Furter, Chorizo, and Guido

"Everyone will smile at you," my friend Ben warned me before I left for Milwaukee. "It's creepy. But don't be alarmed."

It's good that I went in prepared. I don't want to generalize about an entire region, but in my admittedly limited experience, those stereotypes about friendly, kind, open midwesterners exist for good reason. The people of Milwaukee could not have been nicer to me.

Naturally, this made me uncomfortable.

I followed the Mets to Milwaukee for a game at the tail end of July 2007, to watch Tom Glavine go for his three hundredth win. Glavine, the first player I ever interviewed, had struck me as a friendly, thoughtful, down-to-earth guy, and he took the time to treat me like an actual professional, back before I *felt* like a professional. I'm positive that Glavine wouldn't remember me in the slightest, but I'll certainly remember him. After nearly single-handedly costing the Mets the division on the last day of the 2007 season, Glavine is no longer what you'd call popular at Shea, but I'll always think fondly of him.

The Brewers are the smallest-market team in all of baseball by most measures (Milwaukee proper has about a fifth of the population of just Brooklyn alone), and since they play in the middle of the country—an area I'd never even set foot in, unless you count Las Vegas, which you probably shouldn't—I figured Milwaukee would provide a sharp contrast to the Yankee and Met experience.

And it did. The Brewers played well for much of the '07 season and their fans are informed and enthusiastic, but Miller Park was like an alien landscape. Clean, pretty, friendly, it was a pleasant experience all around . . . except that, like a lot of people who've spent their lives in and around New York City, I find being surrounded by the kindness of midwesterners a little disconcerting.

Let me just say here that I understand why people from other parts of the country get annoyed with New Yorkers' refusal to see their city as anything other than the center of the world. It's obnoxious and dismissive, this attitude toward the rest of America, grudging respect for L.A. and (maybe, sometimes) Chicago aside. There are lots of great cities in the United States and plenty of sophisticated people between the coasts.

That said . . . come on. If New York isn't the center of the world, what is?

But Milwaukee is, from what I saw, a lovely city. Its residents are proud of it and mostly unconcerned with whether the world revolves around them or not. I don't think I got an unkind look or word from anyone the entire time I was there (only about forty-eight hours, granted, but that's plenty of time to rack up unkind looks in New York). It's a real city, but still I kept thinking of an exchange from the nineties sitcom *NewsRadio*:

> PHIL: Every day we deal with crime, murder—you're not in
> Wisconsin, Dave. The big story isn't about a cow wandering
> into the town square.
> DAVE: Phil, you know I worked in Milwaukee. It's a city with
> a population of a million people.
> PHIL: So that must have been quite a hubbub when that cow
> got loose.

The kindness started on the plane, a short and uneventful flight, when I was seated next to a pleasant-looking lawyer with snowy hair—he must have been in his sixties, or close to it, but looked younger—who wasted little time in introducing himself as Ralph. We had a lively conversation that made the flight pass quickly; he was a

Brewers fan, though a casual one, but our talk ran from Bud Selig's somewhat sordid past as Milwaukee's owner, to litigation's role in society, to Ralph's daughters and grandchildren. When he found out I was making my first trip to Milwaukee he sprang into action and drew me a map on a scrap of paper, showing the route from my hotel to the nearby river walk, complete with annotated sights and recommended restaurants. I used it, too, the next day; Ralph exuded reliability and sanity.

He'd gone to a Subway Series game at Shea a few years back, he told me, and was struck by the fans' intensity. He especially remembered a man—a *grown man,* he specified—in a Jeter jersey, who, after the Yankee captain got a big hit, stood up and screamed and pointed at the name on the back of his shirt.

"Yes?" I prompted, assuming there was more to this story—that the man had then been punched in the mouth by a Mets fan, or tumbled out of his seat and crushed the unfortunate people seated a few rows below, something along those lines. Otherwise, this seemed to me like pointing out that a lake has a fish in it.

"It's like he thought *he* somehow deserved credit for the hit," marveled Ralph.

This is a part of fan culture I've come to take so completely for granted that I generally don't even notice it anymore. I'm sure there are fans in Milwaukee who do this, too, fans everywhere do this. Taking completely unjustified pride in your team's success is part of the fun, your reward for deigning to support these bums. So I think Ralph's surprise was more a function of his casual fandom than any rationality on the part of Brewers fans . . . but then again, I really didn't see much of that sort of thing at the ballpark the next night. Perhaps they just save it for the Packers.

We continued chatting as we deplaned, trekked through the airport (which features a large used-book store—that's when I knew I was going to like Milwaukee), and gathered our luggage. At which point Ralph explained that he would happily offer me a ride to my hotel, but his wife wasn't going to pick him up for another half hour, so if I preferred to get a taxi rather than wait, the cab stand was right over there.

He meant it, too—he absolutely would have been glad to give me a ride. And while there's no way I ever could overcome decades of training and actually accept, I'm sure that it would have been completely fine if I had—not just fine but really pleasant.

Anyone who accepted a ride from a stranger at a New York airport . . . well, you never want to blame the victim, but pieces of that person would be found in the Gowanus Canal days later and most people would shake their heads and invoke Darwinism.

Miller Park, built in 2001, is a striking building, tall and imposing with a deliberately industrial aspect that's aesthetically very cool, though also sort of jarring given the pastoral, old-fashioned claptrap with which baseball is usually surrounded. I guess at this point in American history, actual factories are scarce enough to inspire nostalgia. The dome was open for this game—it can close in just ten minutes—and it was a beautiful evening, warm and clear, the evening sunlight catching the building's many panes of glass and leaving strange patterns on the stands. The ballpark, as Ralph had explained to me, was controversial in the city when it was built, over the objections of a majority of citizens, and there were still hard feelings. Some things are the same everywhere.

Miller Park is famous for its tailgates as much as its baseball, and in wandering around its parking lots before the game—parking lots roughly the size of Queens—I doubt I took in even 10 percent of the party. There was a game I've never seen before involving tossing beanbags into a small target hole, elaborate grilling setups and spreads, and Porta-Potties. This was a weeknight, too. Neither the Yankees nor the Mets look kindly on tailgating, and while people still find a way—Americans will always, always find a way to get their beer in; we are a resourceful people—half the fans aren't driving to the game anyway. This reminded me more of the scene outside Giants Stadium on game days in the fall.

The team employees were plentiful and polite and wouldn't have lasted three seconds in a steel cage match with the tough old crew at Yankee Stadium. The concession stands were well located and the lines quick-moving, and they sold fried cheese curds (not as gross as they sound, but still kind of gross) and the Brewers' famous variety of sausages, with their closely guarded "secret stadium sauce," which is also sold in the team store. Milwaukee takes its sausages very, very seriously.

As is the case almost everywhere, there are things that work about Miller Park and things that don't quite. Bernie Brewer is a perfectly fine mascot, for instance, but he's been defanged. He appears on a platform above left field during games, and he used to dive down a spiral slide into a huge beer mug. These days, given concerns about the appropriateness of a children's mascot being so tied to alcohol, Bernie slides down the spiral into nothing at all. (I mean, he's a *brewer*. What are kids supposed to assume he's brewing?)

After the first inning of this particular game, Bernie appeared— heralded by loud fireworks that made me jump about a foot out of my seat—for an odd little game: he dropped balls (soft ones, I can only hope) from his perch high over left field, and below him a young boy tried to catch them on a large fake pizza. If he caught a certain number of balls, as near as I could tell, his whole section won free sausage. I wish I could have been at the meeting where they came up with that one.

My absolute favorite thing about Milwaukee fans was their indifference to the free T-shirts that are periodically shot into the crowd. Well, *indifference* is the wrong word—people clapped and grabbed for the shirts. But in New York, at Shea and at Madison Square Garden, these moments are all too often the loudest the crowd will ever get. I've never really understood the fascination—sure, it's free, but it's also a cheap, ugly shirt that's no doubt XXL and won't fit anyway.

If one comes at you, by all means catch it, but the yelling, pleading, and arm-waving always struck me as undignified. So I was thrilled that Milwaukee fans saved their enthusiasm for the really important thing: the sausage race.

I try to play it off like my love of the sausage race is ironic and knowing, but it isn't really: I just think it's awesome. Why five people donning giant hot dog costumes and dashing around the bases should make me so happy, I can't imagine, but it does. There are a number of rip-offs now—the Nationals' racing presidents, Pittsburgh's sad little pierogies, Tampa Bay's downright insulting competition between different brands of PepsiCo soft drinks (Pepsi versus Aquafina versus Sierra Mist). Pale imitations.

Prior to my trip I was unaware of the fact that the racing sausages have names. The bratwurst, in lederhosen, is Brett Wurst. The Polish sausage, which for reasons that elude me wears sunglasses, is Stosh. The baseball-capped hot dog is Frankie Furter, and the chorizo, added in 2006 in a real only-in-America attempt at multiculturalism and wearing a sombrero, is called Cinco. The Italian sausage, dressed as a chef, is called . . . wait for it . . . Guido.

This particular night the game would go thirteen innings, so the Brewers held a *second* sausage race, this one after the twelfth inning, which made my entire night. It left me with a warm, contented glow that lingered even after the thirteenth inning, when I realized I'd just traveled a thousand miles to watch Aaron Sele blow a game.

The Brewers' other entertainment choices don't hold a candle to the sausage race, but then, few things do. "Roll Out the Barrel" is a great song to play during the seventh-inning stretch, and so superior to the Yankees' choice of the tacky and irrelevant "Cotton-Eyed Joe" that it doesn't even bear discussing. There's a lot of stuff in the lyrics about gardens and happy faces and sweet romancing and the polka that all feels very far from New York, with a charming old-timey chorus:

Roll out the barrel, we'll have a barrel of fun
Roll out the barrel, we've got the blues on the run

Zing, boom, tararrel, sing out a song of good cheer
Now's the time to roll the barrel, for the gang's all here!

(I like Shea's bouncy "Lazy Mary" tarantella, too, but given that the lyrics are all in Italian it's never going to be much of a sing-along.)

I found the Brewers fans knowledgeable, which was great, and also respectful, which was odd. They gave Glavine an enthusiastic round of applause when he walked off the field in the seventh inning with a one-run lead, in line for his three hundredth career win. It was a classy gesture, given that their team was losing at the time. I tried to remember instances when New York fans had done something similar—surely there have been a few such occasions, when some momentous achievement overwhelmed team loyalty. I'm drawing a blank, though. I think it would depend on the day—maybe I've been part of crowds that could conceivably behave graciously under the right circumstances, I don't know, but I've definitely been part of crowds that would've happily thrown batteries at Ted Williams's head while he tried to hit .400 on the last day of the season, given the chance.

The couple to my right, plump and in their fifties, had driven in for the game from a small town several hours away. Longtime Brewers fans, they clapped not just for Glavine—the man nodding for emphasis—but also after an impressive piece of hitting by any Mets batter.

I left my seat in the late innings, after the Mets bullpen blew the lead—of course they did—and flitted around Miller Park, from the highest seat (really, really high, actually) back down to the clubhouse stores and bathrooms. The whole place was just remarkably clean. I would have felt completely comfortable sitting on the floor on any one of their main levels, whereas when the bottom of my jeans touched the floor at Shea, even briefly, I had to fight the urge to go home and burn them. Once I left Shea in a pounding downpour after a Braves game was rained out and I'd made the mistake of wearing flip-flops; I had to wade through inches of foul water both inside the building and outside it, on the way to the 7 train, where in the fluo-rescent light I could watch the brown gunk covering my feet slow dry and begin flaking off. Like everyone's friendliness, this Milwaukee tidiness was only a good thing, but not the trappings I'm used to at a ball game. Even most of the Mets fans I spotted, perhaps cowed by their environs, were calm and respectful.

It was by the smoking area, naturally, that I finally found a bit of New York atmosphere. Two guys in their early to mid-twenties were walking toward the doors, getting their cigarettes out. They were both wearing black Mets jerseys—Martinez and Piazza—but I knew they were from New York before I turned around to see that. The accent was unmistakable and, along with it, the sentiment:

"I'm telling you," the guy in the Martinez jersey was saying, hold-ing out a flat upraised hand to fend off interruption—"no, man, *I'm telling you,* Derek Jeter is a *fucking faggot,* man."

Ah, I thought. *Feels like home.*

After the game I headed toward the bus loop, past a line of wait-ing taxis, and found the line for service back downtown; the buses didn't normally run this late, but they'd been held till the end of the game. The trip was surprisingly easy—I'd been expecting to have to grab a cab—and made more so by the fact that the main concourse of Miller Park was sprinkled with Brewers employees who were not only willing but downright thrilled to be helpful. There's no easy parallel to be drawn at Yankee Stadium—even I don't know where the hell buses stop around there, though it's not like you could miss the subway—but the general sense I got was that the Brewers employees were ready to go above and beyond to assist fans with whatever they might need, whereas the average employee at Shea or Yankee Stadium (as-suming you could find one) might or might not stop to give you water if you were dying of thirst in the upper deck. If they did, it wouldn't be with a smile. And they'd charge you five bucks for it.

Anyway, the bus filled up quickly with tired fans, many in Mets jerseys—a disproportionate number, less likely than the average Brewers fan to have a car with them. The man in a Glavine jersey who sat down next to me, though, said he'd driven all the way from Long Island for this one (though he bused to the game in order to drink). He wanted to be there when Glavine got number three hundred, he said, because it was "history being made," and also because "the guy's a class act."

(I thought about this guy—a fellow New Yorker, we did not exchange names—at the end of the season, wondering if he was railing at Glavine like so many other fans or if, having driven all the way to Wisconsin and back, he would be too invested in his positive image of the pitcher to change his attitude. He planned to drive back to the city the next morning, so he didn't make it to Chicago, and never got to see Glavine finally get his three hundredth.)

After all the seats had filled, a deeply, deeply drunk college student in a Brewers jersey climbed on and blearily took in the situation. He was holding on to a pole as if it were the only thing keeping him upright, probably because it was.

"There are too many Mets fans on this bus," he bellowed in the general direction of the man sitting next to me and the clusters of New York jerseys behind us. "Don't let any more Mets fans on! What's with all the Mets fans?"

Here we go, I thought, smiling. *This is more like it.* Drunk idiots are the same all over, right? But then he continued: "Aw, I'm just playing, man. Hey, you from New York? Welcome to Milwaukee!"

He was smiling now, and sloppily stuck his hand out for the Long Island Glavine fan to shake, which the Long Islander did, though warily.

"Hey," slurred the college student, "that Jose Reyes can really play, huh?"

Twenty minutes later, we were back downtown, the streets deserted though it couldn't have been much past midnight, stores and restaurants closed, except for the occasional bar on a side street. The

Brewers fan started up again; I was still waiting for him to turn belligerent.

"Everybody get off at First Street—there's a party at the Ale House! And you're all invited! Well, except for Mets fans."

Pause . . .

"Unless you want to come—then you're invited, too! Especially if you're buying the drinks."

Pause . . .

"But even if you aren't! No, seriously, it's going to be awesome, you should totally come."

I don't want to exaggerate too much here, because it's not like Brewers fans at Shea would have been attacked and chased through the streets. They might have a few insults hurled at them, sure, but if they were behaving politely—and they *definitely* would be behaving politely—they might not. (Though I do have an Orioles fan friend who was once actually spat on for wearing a Brian Roberts jersey to the Stadium, and this after the Yankees had won the game.) Plenty of people would be happy to help them locate their seats, and if they needed help figuring out the subway, I'm sure someone would step up with directions. Still, it's a different experience.

Objectively, it's hard to argue that Miller Park isn't on the whole a more pleasant, affordable, and civilized place to catch a game than either of the old New York ballparks. Better seats for far less money, easier to get to, cleaner, and almost completely without hostility. And yet . . . (You know what's coming, right? Sure you do.) I'd still take the nutcases and dirt of the New York stadiums any day, even if they come with $9 beers and inane security lines.

Maybe this is just a stubborn attempt to justify blind loyalty to the things I find familiar and normal, but for me, the fact that baseball in New York is a bit of a fight—getting there, fighting crowds, dealing with grime and with assholes—makes the baseball itself that much more rewarding. Sort of like the city itself, right? It's overpriced and overcrowded and inconvenient, and every so often someone spits on you, but people keep coming anyway. It takes an irrational amount of effort to live here, but if you can put up with it, it's that much more of a victory.

Or maybe that's all bullshit. Maybe I'm crazy to live here when I could move to some perfectly lovely smaller city and live in a two-bedroom instead of a minute studio and not get trampled on the subway daily. Maybe the above paragraph is just an elaborate, deluded justification. It doesn't really matter, because it's too late for me: New York is home now.

Regardless, I maintain there was an energy at Shea and at Yankee Stadium during a great game that's hard to find elsewhere. Maybe it's only because the people of Milwaukee are too sane to duplicate it, or maybe New Yorkers are just drawing on the larger energy of the city itself. Whatever the cause, I wouldn't trade it for anything.

Okay, except for the sausage race. I'd totally trade it for that.

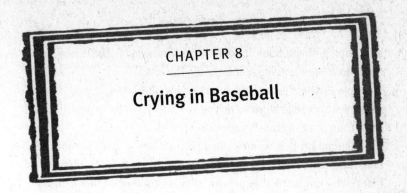

CHAPTER 8

Crying in Baseball

In the middle of the 2008 season Linda, the Mets fan I met at Shea when we both donated our blood for free Mets tickets, got us bleacher seats to a Mets–Rangers game at Shea, through some sort of Fox News promotion the Mets had going with the show *Fox & Friends*. I leapt at the ticket, not just because it was free but because you generally couldn't just buy a bleacher seat at Shea; they were reserved for groups, so I'd never sat there. Before the game they had giveaways, including a fire-truck-red Fox News hat (which, in New York City the summer before the 2008 election, I wasn't able to give away even as a joke), a fairly decent buffet, even free beer.

They also had information available about another promotion coming up later in the summer: Take Her Out to the Ballgame, a variation on Ladies' Night. The team would be giving tote bags with Palmer's Cocoa Butter lotion samples to the first twenty-five thousand female fans, and as the perky flyer explained, there would be a panel on how to better understand baseball.

My knee-jerk reaction was annoyance—the team was assuming that girls need to have the game explained to them and would best be lured in with cosmetics and bags instead of action on the field. Lots of teams have, or at one point had, a similar night; in fact, these promotions have been going on since the nineteenth century. The Washington Nationals' was a big hit a few years ago, with massages, manicures, and Mary Kay cosmetics. Both the Nationals and the Mets sold copies of the book *It Takes More Than Balls: The Savvy Girls' Guide to Understanding and Enjoying Baseball.*

Now, I haven't read this book, so for all I know, it may be awesome. Cal Ripken Jr. blurbs it on the Savvy Girls' website, which is a lot more than I can say for *this* book. But the idea of it bugs me—not just the assumption that women need help understanding baseball, but that they should read some separate book especially targeted at them. Why not just write, or read, a guide to understanding and enjoying baseball, period? The Savvy Girls talk about how there's no wrong way to be a baseball fan, which I agree with, but they also say they have a different perspective than their "male counterparts"—for example, "We certainly didn't compare stats from decades ago between players who were dead." Yes, because everyone knows girls think numbers are gross! (Or, as Teen Talk Barbie so famously put it in my youth, "Math class is *hard.*") They also promise to answer probing questions like "Just what's with these confounding player salaries, anyway?" which makes it seem like the target audience is not women but children.

Anyway, after I'd worked up a good head of steam about Take Her Out to the Ballgame, I was forced to admit that, in fact, the Mets have a point: while there are millions of knowledgeable female fans out there, women are still a relative minority. And a lot of them, including plenty of my friends, *are* more interested in cocoa butter than curveballs.

Gender differences are a minefield of a topic, and I want to tread carefully because in many areas I have no idea myself how much they're genetic, how much they're a product of cultural or societal conditioning, and how much they're myths. Are women inherently, biologically less likely to enjoy baseball than men are? Or are they less interested in it because society expects them to be and doesn't condition them to watch sports the way it does men? Is it some combination of those two factors? You could argue these points forever—but I'm not even sure the baseball gender gap is as huge as people tend to think.

Many studies over the last decade or so, of varying reliability and scientific soundness, have attempted to find out just who baseball fans are. One found that 37 percent of American women identify themselves as baseball fans (compared to 49 percent of men); another poll had it at 44 percent to 66 percent but included those who said they "somewhat" followed baseball, which could mean just about anything, including vaguely noting the back-page headline of the *New York Post* on the subway each morning. Yet another study showed 51 percent of women calling themselves fans. Even if we assume for the sake of argument that the lower number is closer to the truth, 37 percent is nothing to sneeze at.

Meanwhile, a Scarborough Research report back in 2004 found that 42 percent of all baseball fans are women. And a 2002 Gallup poll found that while the percentage of men who call themselves baseball fans has been decreasing for decades, the percentage of women who say the same is holding steady. So yes, there are certainly more male than female baseball fans, but the chasm isn't as wide as it's usually represented to be.

You can tell a lot about what kind of audience a given TV show expects by paying attention to the commercials. I've spent thousands of hours watching baseball, which means I've sat through countless thirty-second spots for razors, hair regrowth serum, erectile-dysfunction pills, and beer ads showing guys choosing Coors Light over women. There must be nearly an hour of ads during a typical Mets or Yankees broadcast, if not more, and often not a single spot is targeted at me. I used to get a small pseudo-subversive kick out of how I was throwing a wrench into all these marketing strategies—*Ha! I am immune to your marketing efforts, motherfuckers! I will* not *ask my doctor about prostate enlargement!*—but then I just bought a TiVo, which is better.

Lest you think I'm being too hard on the Savvy Girls and their pink-splashed *Guide to Understanding and Enjoying Baseball,* it's indeed occurred to me that maybe men and women do tend to watch the game a bit differently. For one thing, I've never played baseball, not even softball. So I don't have that kind of connection to the game, which many guys I know seem to feel, even if they never got past Little League. And I've become plenty interested in statistics, but there's no pretending that was any large part of what drew me to the game initially, or that it has much to do with why I keep watching (though the same could be said of plenty of men). I do accumulate baseball numbers in my brain, like most fans, and I enjoy doing so. I have a recurring fantasy in which someone desperately needs to know, say, the modern record for most wins by a pitcher in a single season, he's absolutely frantic about it, and I get to finally use the information that's been rattling around in my head for years and years: I turn to the guy and calmly inform him it was 41 Ws, Happy Jack Chesbro, 1904. (It's going to happen any day now.) But no, numbers aren't what sucked me in and they're not what keep me here.

When I first got interested in baseball, and stopped treating it as background noise and actually focused on it, it was the characters that drew me in, the personalities, and the drama, more than any inherent beauty of the game. I didn't really care what kind of pitch someone threw or whether a batter had shortened his swing; I just wanted to see if Paul O'Neill was going to be beating himself up all night, cursing his perceived failures in the dugout, terrorizing innocent water coolers. I wanted to see how the rookie replacing Tony Fernandez might overcome what I assumed had to be a bad case of nerves and succeed in the big leagues. I wanted Bernie Williams to do well because I wanted a shy, awkward dude with glasses to win one for shy, awkward people with glasses everywhere.

Jerry Seinfeld famously said that rooting for a sports team in the modern era is "rooting for laundry"—players come and go so frequently, and are so often mercenary dicks while they're here, that we end up just cheering for the team as an entity, as embodied by whoever happens to be wearing its uniform at the time. It's hard to argue with the basic truth of that (Johnny Damon in a red and white jersey is loathed; six months later he puts on a blue and white shirt and is hailed as a hero). But for me, especially in the beginning, it wasn't the case. I was very much rooting for the individuals.

Maybe it's easier for kids to do that because they aren't yet fully aware of the transience and foibles of professional athletes. I don't remember any disillusioning moment in particular—no single arrest or defection or painfully incoherent interview that made me realize these guys aren't capital-*H* heroes off the field and it's pointless and foolish to look at them that way. Certainly it became clear over time, the more I read and watched, that many players were people I would not have much in common with. But you know, even after all this time, with countless DUIs and lakes of steroids in the rearview mirror, it doesn't really matter. It's still the drama and the personalities that draw me to the game, and just because players don't always display winning personalities, that doesn't make them less interesting. And I know full well by now that those personalities are mostly just a fan and/or media projection, but that doesn't seem to make much difference, either. I know a soap opera isn't real, but that doesn't mean I don't want to find out what happens when Erica's evil twin sleeps with her ex-husband.

Whether or not there's anything inherently female about this perspective, a lot of mainstream male sportswriters (at least a lot of my favorites) tend to eschew this kind of stuff. They try to rise above the tabloid fray and don't spend much time on character or colorful shenanigans, taking the view that what's measurable on the field is all that deserves our attention. Intellectually, I can't disagree, especially because if you're a journalist you want to try to stick to the facts, and your own take on the people involved is too much a constructed story line. Still, those story lines are what I find most fascinating, which is why I'd rather watch a meaningless, sloppy game involving a team I know well than a well-played high-stakes match between two teams I rarely watch. I certainly find baseball interesting in and of itself, but if I'm not familiar with the people involved, however inaccurate that perceived familiarity might be, it becomes a bit of an empty exercise.

I'm not so sure this is a gender issue. Take A-Rod (please). There's plenty to watch and analyze and discuss in his game: his power, his batting eye, his fielding, his baserunning, all the skills responsible for his iconic status. But there's no way he'd be taking up literally hundreds of tabloid front and back pages a year if baseball fans—or really, human beings in general—didn't love amateur psychoanalysis.

I've seen plenty of burly fortysomething men launch into an examination of the intricate emotional ties, betrayals, and day-by-day minutiae in the relationship between Derek Jeter and Alex Rodriguez with a depth that would make fifteen-year-old girls blush. I don't want to read too much into lowest-common-denominator sports talk radio, where that kind of conversation is especially prevalent, but lots of baseball discussion is, at base, gossip. "I hear that Joe Torre said that A-Rod said . . . and Delgado *never* liked Willie Randolph . . . and, oh my God, did you hear about Carl Pavano and his girlfriend?"

"Yeah, and did you see that photo, A-Rod's lips, are like purple!"

"I think he wears lip gloss!"

"Ew! And that stripper said he likes butch chicks . . ."

I guess it's a fine line between the character-based stuff I find interesting and conversations that sound like those at an especially nasty middle school cafeteria table. I'm sure I go over that line myself sometimes. But sports give adults, and maybe men in particular, license to behave in ways that are usually off-limits, and might even seem kinda girly.

When many people think about girls and baseball, they think of *A League of Their Own* and of its oft-quoted line: "Are you crying? There's no crying! There's no crying in baseball!" It's a nice bit of dialogue but wildly untrue: baseball is full of grown men crying.

Joe Torre, a sixtysomething tough former catcher and Brooklyn native, wept on national television nearly every fall for a decade. Kyle Farnsworth, of all people, who walked around the clubhouse in camo tank tops reading gun magazines, teared up on camera when the Yankees traded him. Some players cry when they make the playoffs and some cry when they don't. They cry when they win the World Series and they cry when they lose the ALCS in seven games. And the fans— the fans cry, too. In fact, for a certain kind of crusty older guy, a Mets playoff win might well constitute one of very few legitimate opportunities to shed tears without shame.

I have seen dozens if not hundreds of men cry over baseball. My dad never did, at least that I saw, though when he was a kid the Red Sox produced tears on more than one occasion. I myself have never exactly *cried* about baseball, but I've gotten a little misty a few times:

- In the fall of 2001, when the Mets beat the Braves in the first New York home game since 9/11, on a come-from-behind Mike Piazza home run—though that was, of course, not really about baseball. The game was just the instigator. But I guess that's often the case when people cry over sports.

- Later in 2001, during the Yankees' playoff run, repeatedly. The main moment came in Game 5 of the World Series, Yankees versus Diamondbacks, when the crowd said goodbye to my beloved Paul O'Neill, who would be retiring after the Series. It was the top of the ninth, the Yankees were trailing, and the fans knew that if the Yanks didn't rally, it might be their last chance to serenade O'Neill out in left field. They chanted his name, over and over again, for what felt like forever, though really it was only a few minutes. O'Neill was looking around nervously, unsure of how to react, and trying to focus in case he had to make a play; finally, on his long walk back to the dugout, he tipped his cap and started tearing up himself, which turned me into a pile of mush. Later he said that what amazed him the most was that the team was losing at the time (they did come back later, almost miraculously, for the second game in a row, of course causing me to tear up again). Yeah, Yankees fans can be entitled jerks sometimes, but that one particular moment was classy as hell.

- 2004 ALCS, Game 7.

I'm not proud of that last one. It's one thing to get misty with joy when your team wins, but to start sniffling when they lose—if you're older than twelve or so—is a little pathetic. What can I say? It was the Red Sox. The Yankees were beginning to lose their aura of invincibility by 2004, but I still knew, deep in my soul, that no matter what might go wrong for them, they would never lose a playoff series to the *Red Sox*. Not that I ever bought into all that "curse of the Bambino" nonsense, but by that point, especially after the 2003 ALCS, it really was starting to seem like Yankee dominance over the Sox was some kind of law of nature, or at least the product of a genuine Boston mental block. Plus, teams just don't come back to win a Series after going down 3–0; the odds against the Sox were overwhelming.

To make matters worse—and this is something I haven't admitted to many people—the Sox victory was basically my fault. I don't believe in jinxes . . . except in baseball, and I jinxed the heck out of the Yankees that fall. I'd gone to Ticketmaster.com and, after much desperate reloading, bought myself a ticket to a possible Game 6 at the Stadium. I'd never been to a Championship Series game and I was beyond excited: Red Sox–Yankees in the playoffs, at the Stadium, a likely instant classic. So as the Yankees were celebrating their third straight win over Boston in Game 3, I turned to my then-roommate— my Red Sox fan roommate, no less—and actually said out loud, "I kind of wish the Yankees would lose a couple, so I could use my ticket! Then I might even get to see them clinch."

Even now, remembering that moment, I wince. It's like driving up the BQE and exclaiming over the lack of traffic, which inevitably leads to a massive jam materializing within half a mile. Logically you know that your words had no impact on the situation, but in your mind they'll always be linked—especially true in sports fandom, which is a remarkably superstitious culture. (There are far more old wives' tales in sports than among actual elderly wives.)

In any case, the tension went out of Game 7 early, in the second inning, when grumpy old man Kevin Brown left the bases loaded and Johnny Damon (then on the Sox) hit a grand slam off Brown's hapless replacement, Javier Vasquez. (Note that this is also the moment when a large group of Yankee fans stopped implicitly trusting Joe Torre, adding a sense of Oedipal betrayal to the general shame.) My eyes actually got a little damp as the realization sank in; the rest of the game was a long and painful death rattle. None of my roommates was home at the time, to my relief, and I was talking to my dad on the phone.

"Turn it off," he said. "There's no reason for you to watch this. I'll call you if they start to come back."

So I shut off the TV, went into my room, and tried to read—I can't remember what, because I was so distracted that I'd get to the bottom of a page before realizing I hadn't actually absorbed a single word of it. My dad called multiple times, and I'd leap to pick up the phone:

"Hey, are they coming back?"

"No. A-Rod just grounded out."

"Oh—I thought maybe there was a rally."

"No, they're going down without a fight. I'll call you if they get something going."

Ten minutes later, the phone would ring again.

"Are they coming back?!"

"No. This is awful."

I did turn it back on in time to watch the last inning—it seemed unsportsmanlike not to. And I teared up again just a little. It was petulant and immature, especially considering that the Yankees had won their fourth World Series in five years just a few years before, and I was glad no one was there to see it. I haven't come anywhere near crying over baseball since, and can't really imagine doing so again, at least not over a loss. I don't know if that's because now the worst (baseball-wise) has already happened, or because I've just grown up, or because writing about the team professionally took the edge off my partisan passion. Probably some combination.

I've gotten off track here. The point is that baseball as a culture is full to the gills of crying, with men at least as likely as women to have an irrational emotional reaction about their team. When the Mets lost the last game of the 2007 season, fans of all genders and ages cried in the stands.

In fact, I think this is one of sports' societal functions: it gives grown men an emotional outlet. Men crying about trouble at work or in a relationship are still sometimes seen (by idiots) as weak or effeminate. Crying about sports, once in a while anyway, is acceptably masculine.

I remember a study from one of my long-ago anthropology classes, which theorized that while women tend to bond with each other by sharing information—talking, exchanging news and confidences—men tend to bond instead via shared experiences, by *doing* things together. (Note that while I signed up for several anthro courses naively imagining that they would explain human nature to me, a decent amount of what we read was the usual subjective theories and inconclusive speculation of so much liberal arts education, so I'm not sure how seriously to take this finding. Obviously it's an oversimplification, but I don't think it's totally baseless.) Girls get together all the time just to talk, but guys often look for an activity to talk around, and a game is perfect for that.

Whether or not it's typically masculine behavior, I've certainly bonded with people of both genders through baseball on many occasions. The friends I've made through baseball are often those I have least in common with otherwise; we start out talking so much about the Yankees or Mets that it might be months or years before they mention casually that they have thrown out all their "secular music."

_____

You'd think being a huge baseball fan would come in handy when dating, but for the most part, I can't say that's been the case. I don't know if there's a reason, or if it's just the luck of the draw, but most of the guys I've gone out with haven't been huge fans. Which is fine, but it does lead to a lot of conversations along the following lines:

BF: Want to try out that new Colombian restaurant on Fifth and then check out the new Jim Jarmusch movie?
ME: Are you crazy? The Yanks–Sox game is on tonight!

TiVo has helped.

I did have one date with a massive baseball fan who equaled my obsessiveness. It happened while I was working as a copywriter, and my coworker—a very sweet person, despite her propensity for setting up blind dates—kept telling me how much I had in common with her roommate, whom I'll call Bob. I met him one day when he stopped by the office, and a few days later she suggested we hang out some time and put us in touch. We agreed to watch a spring training game together at a sports bar on Third Avenue.

Now, it turned out that by "you have *so much* in common" my friend pretty much just meant we both loved baseball. Bob was a huge Cleveland Indians fan. He was also a perfectly nice guy, and not bad-looking, with a job in public radio, but we just didn't have much of a connection, and conversation tended to snag if we drifted too far from baseball.

I don't remember how it came up, but eventually the talk turned to Derek Jeter's defense. Like any red-blooded American male from outside the tri-state area, Bob hated the Yankees with a searing passion, so he was being a little uncharitable, but I was compelled to agree with him on one salient point: that Derek Jeter's defense had been overrated for years and was swiftly moving from poor to awful. Pretty much everyone knows this now, but it was a bit more of a niche viewpoint then. I'd already been convinced, since virtually every rep-utable defensive metric had Jeter ranked toward the very bottom of the league, and once I had time to get used to the idea, I could see it myself—how many balls shot "past a diving Jeter" and into the out-field, when other team's shortstops had no trouble making similar plays.

However, I didn't appreciate Bob's venomous tone. Derek Jeter's defense sucks, but Derek Jeter, as an overall player, certainly does not . . . and anyway, I couldn't just let some *Indians* fan talk about him like that.

So in a slightly roundabout defense of the captain, I pointed out that despite being generally a poor defensive shortstop, he'd made a few really excellent plays in big moments. There was the time the pre-vious summer when he'd jumped over the Stadium railing and into the crowd while catching a pop fly against the Red Sox and came up bat-tered and bleeding but with the ball. And of course, most memorably, there was the "flip play," in Game 3 of the 2001 Division Series, against the Oakland Athletics.

To recap: the Yankees are down 2–0 in the series, facing elimina-tion in a tight one-run game. It's the seventh inning, and Jeremy Giambi—who makes his brother Jason look like a gazelle—is on first. Terrence Long doubles to right, and Yankee right fielder Shane Spencer frantically hurls the ball toward home plate, but it's a lousy throw and misses not one but two cut-off men, trickling down the first-base line. Suddenly, out of nowhere—and every description of this play ever written includes the phrase "out of nowhere"—Derek Jeter swoops into view, across the diamond from where any rational person would expect him to be, and in one motion scoops the ball up and shovels it to Jorge Posada, who tags Jeremy Giambi on the shin with a fraction of a second to spare. The A's don't score, and the Yan-kees go on to win 1–0.

Really, this might as well be called the "why the fuck didn't Jeremy Giambi slide play" instead of the "Jeter flip play," but it was nevertheless remarkable. Jeter insisted afterward that the Yankees practiced that play in spring training, which actually turned out to be true. Still, no one could recall seeing anything quite like it before, and no one has since. There's just no way in hell you could have expected Derek Jeter to make that play—no way he should have been there to get to the ball in time, let alone pull off that lightning-fast toss to Posada. Anyway, talking to Bob after a few afternoon beers, I held up this moment as one sparkling gem on Jeter's otherwise unimpressive defensive resume.

"Nah," said Bob. "That play's so overrated. Watch it again—you'll see, Giambi was going to be out anyway."

There are a lot of things I'm unsure of in this world—the meaning of human existence, how to properly clean my George Foreman Grill, why people keep guinea pigs as pets—but I do know, without the slightest doubt, that this is bullshit. No way Jeremy Giambi is out if Jeter isn't there, making a crazy out-of-position play, nor is he out if Jeter doesn't flawlessly execute it. This being a first date, though, tact was called for.

"That's the dumbest thing I've ever heard," I said.

(Unfair of me—it isn't even one of the top five dumbest things I've ever heard. Top ten, maybe.)

We had a fairly heated argument right there in the bar; to my surprise (and considerable embarrassment later, when recounting the story to my friends), I was genuinely ticked off. Bob was, too, his hatred for Derek Jeter apparently being one of the motivating forces in his life. Had things gone a little differently, maybe this could have been an adorable anniversary story to tell people about later. Instead we recovered our composure and chatted awkwardly till the end of the game, then made our excuses and never contacted each other again.

Being a female sportswriter is rarer than being a female fan, and a bit more stressful. There has been vast progress made over the last thirty years, and I very much doubt I would have had the guts to put myself through what some of the first female sportswriters went through in the seventies and eighties. Because of what they and many women since accomplished, I've never had to deal with anything genuinely scary or insulting in a locker room. These days there are just minor awkwardnesses that go with the territory.

It's being extra-careful not to ask a dumb question, because it's that much easier for someone to assume you don't know what you're talking about (this was especially tricky when I covered a Jets or Giants game, because in fact I really *didn't* know what I was talking about; surely my presence was not helpful to the other female reporters there, who did). It's fretting about what the hell you're supposed to wear in a locker room to look your best (such as it is) without seeming unprofessional or drawing the wrong kind of attention, when guys can just throw on a button-down shirt and khakis every day. It's glancing at a player's locker to see if he's available for an interview and finding that his towel is off and he's looking up at *exactly that second* to see you looking at him, and being more limited than male colleagues in when you can go up and talk to a player—how undressed is too undressed? Basically, for one of the few times at any of my many jobs, I felt hyperaware of being female—and much more self-conscious than usual, which is pretty damn self-conscious.

I was touched by how several of the more experienced women covering the teams went out of their way to be helpful and kind when I was a freaked-out novice. Johnette Howard of *Newsday,* for example, who's been writing great stuff since the days when it was a fight just to get into a locker room, told me more than once to let her know if I had any questions, and when I did, she was gracious enough to respond as if they weren't dumb. In fact, every single female reporter I met covering either the Yankees or the Mets was at a bare minimum pleasant, and many went beyond the call of duty. The word "sisterhood" is unbearably cheesy but the idea behind it is not, and here were actual role models living up to the responsibility of that role, which doesn't happen too often in pro sports or anywhere else.

———————

When I first started out at the *Village Voice,* I thought covering sports might be a good way to meet guys—not the players, obviously, but other reporters, at least 85 percent of whom were male. You have to like those kind of odds. It does happen; Lisa Kennelly and Jeremy Cothran covered the Yankees and Mets, respectively, for the *Star-Ledger,* fell in love, and are now engaged. But this didn't turn out to be the norm, at least not for me, as the bulk of the reporters turned out to be both middle-aged and married.

Not all of them saw this as an obstacle. One writer, whose work I'd admired for years, went out of his way to be generous and encouraging. I appreciated it, feeling generally in over my head, and when he offered to talk to me sometime about covering the New York teams I jumped at the chance. The vibe of our conversations did feel a little odd to me, but since he was married and—though not unattractive—old enough to be my father, I brushed that aside and scolded myself for thinking the worst of someone who'd been nothing but kind, and for being egotistical enough to think someone was hitting on me when probably he was just being obliging.

We met at a bar, and I knew I'd been wrong to second-guess my instincts when he started encouraging me to drink more, sitting a bit too close, fishing for compliments on how young he looked, and acting surprised that I knew he had a wife (God bless Google). As a rule, I don't assume any guy is actually pursuing me until I've eliminated all other possibilities, but there wasn't much room for ambiguity here.

The tricky thing about this situation, though, is that he still had never overtly come on to me. No groping, no leering. That he *was* coming on to me seemed obvious, but because it hadn't actually been said, I felt I couldn't say anything myself. How do you turn down someone who hasn't put himself out there for rejection? What was to stop him from saying, *You're nuts, you misread the situation, I was just trying to help out a young reporter*? Or from telling everyone what a crazy, egotistical bitch I was?

In the end I endured an awkward three or four beers that night and left (if college taught me anything, it's how to hold my booze), at which point he brushed the hair out of my face and suggested we see each other again. I said sure, and then proceeded to dodge his repeated calls and make up excuses about being busy. Probably not the best or most mature way to handle it, but I felt trapped. After a few weeks of this he emailed me to schedule another time to meet up, and I didn't reply for several days, unsure of what to write. Then I got another, final email from him, saying only: "I thought you were cooler than this. See you at the ballpark."

Sometimes I wonder a little guiltily if standing out—the unusualness of being a female fan or, especially, baseball writer—is part of what drew me to the sport. There were plenty of times when I would have been overjoyed to see a few more women in the locker room, and plenty of nights when I wished some of my female friends were a bit keener on watching a game with me. I don't think of myself as someone who seeks attention, but once in a while it's fun to see yourself as a little unusual.

When I first started blogging about baseball I posted under the name E. K. Span. I wanted it to be gender neutral so that no one would read my words differently knowing that I was a girl—no one would dismiss me for being female or, conversely, embrace me as part of some sort of sports affirmative action.

I quickly realized, though, that if you want your work to be noticed, you need to stand out, and that while there are thousands of aspiring male baseball writers out there, there's only a relative handful of women. I didn't want to be sold as a girl baseball writer—I was terrified of pink fonts and didn't want to be one of the Savvy Girls with their gender-specific guidebook and their puns about balls. I don't want the Mets to think they need to distribute free lip gloss to lure me to the ballpark. Baseball is baseball, and the game doesn't care if the person watching it has a penis.

That said, watching is one thing, but getting other people to read your thoughts about watching is another. If I had to put up with the advances of married colleagues, the awkwardness of trying to interview a player in his underwear, and the occasional crackpot readers urging me to "get back in the kitchen" (obviously having never tried my cooking), I might as well get something out of it, too.

CHAPTER 9

Baseball Is a Universal Language, So Let's Start Talking

The Taiwan Tourism Bureau ran an ad on ESPN a few years back, usually during late-night/early-morning repeats of *Baseball Tonight*. It begins with an image of Chien-Ming Wang in his Yankees uniform towering, Mothra-like, over a mountain range, as a deep voice intones "Chien-Ming Wang: New York's number one starter. Taiwan's shining glory." (This was before Wang's 2008 injury and 2009 meltdown, when he was one of the Yanks' most effective pitchers.) There are quick flashes of Taipei streets, hot noodles, a skyscraper, a Taiwanese family posing awkwardly for the camera. "Baseball is a universal language, so let's start talking. Chien-Ming Wang, Taiwan's glory . . . This program is brought to you by the Taiwan Tourism Bureau. Taiwan: touch your heart."

After months of watching two baseball games a day (for what I initially thought was going to be a book about the 2007 New York season), the bulk of them in my closet-sized studio apartment, I knew I was deep in a rut. It's not something you can ever complain about, watching baseball incessantly, and not something that deserves a shred of sympathy. Still, I was in a fog: I stayed up till 5:00 a.m. and slept till noon; if it weren't for the changing game schedules, I would have had nothing tying me to a particular day of the week or to the passage of time. When I saw my friends I had almost nothing to talk about besides bullpens and lineups. I felt I needed to do something dramatic, to break myself out of the pattern, to shake things up.

So one day, inspired by one of those 3:00 a.m. ESPN ads, I

booked myself a ticket to Taiwan (touch your heart). Which is how, after a summer of sitting on my futon in Brooklyn watching the Yankees for hours on end, I found myself in Taipei—sitting on a hotel bed and watching the Yankees for hours on end.

The idea had first occurred to me several months earlier. Perhaps unsurprisingly, I was slightly drunk at the time, having bullied several friends into coming with me to a big testosterone-heavy neighborhood sports bar called 200 Fifth for the first Subway Series game of the season. I'd just finished a book by Junwei Yu called *Playing in Isolation,* about the evolution of baseball in Taiwan, and between those stories and all the many tales I'd heard of the island's massive devotion to Chien-Ming Wang, the first Taiwanese player to become a bona fide star in the majors, I couldn't stop talking about how neat it would be to see that culture firsthand. Everyone agreed that it was an awesome but totally impractical idea, and I eventually let it go with an "Oh well, maybe one day."

But the thought stuck with me. It's hard to get much further from New York than Taiwan, as I can tell you with authority after thirty-two-hour trips there and back, and putting half the world between me and my rut was awfully appealing.

Despite Taiwan's distance from the Bronx, you won't find more obsessed Yankee fans anywhere. ESPN Taiwan airs every Yankee game multiple times a day, with only short breaks in between for local sporting events (or, randomly, the X-Games). This is all thanks to Wang, who's become a national icon and seems to carry Taiwan's hopes for international recognition—something that would become pretty important to you, I guess, when no major country on the planet will officially admit that your country is even a country. When Wang pitches, the game is shown and reshown on a loop for twenty-four hours, which has earned ESPN Taiwan the nickname "YESPN," in reference to the Yankees' YES network. As fascinating and layered as the country is—in the best tradition of international travel, where you recognize all the basic elements of life but everything surrounding those basics is different in huge or tiny ways—it may not be the ideal destination for Mets fans.

Some of the glamour of the whole halfway-around-the-world thing is offset by the highly unglamorous process of actually getting there. I left my Brooklyn apartment at five on a Sunday morning and arrived in Taipei around ten Monday night, though with all the time changes and the date line crossing and the layovers in L.A. and Tokyo I lost track of exactly how many hours I'd actually been on the road. The Taipei airport (until recently Chiang-Kai Shek International) is about a forty minute drive from the city, so I'd arranged to have a driver from the hotel pick me up, and I was greeted after the luggage carousel by a driver holding a large cardboard sign for "Enna Span." A tiny and energetic uniformed woman ran around with what appeared to be a bomb-sniffing beagle, as "Back That Ass Up" played over the speakers.

Unable to sleep on even a thirteen-hour plane ride, having sat painfully awake through no fewer than four crappy movies, I fell soundly asleep shortly before the car crossed into Taipei. So it wasn't until the next morning that I got a good look at Taipei's most distinctive features: wide boulevards lined with large, blocky buildings, all featuring covered walkways to protect against the frequent rain and thick tropical heat, and broken up by narrow, twisty numbered lanes (off of which spring even narrower, twistier numbered alleys). I'd never traveled in Asia before, and it was those countless tiny back streets that felt truly exotic and made me believe I was really somewhere new. Thousands of mopeds and scooters careened terrifyingly around the streets at all times, observing few if any traffic laws, or even physics laws. If accidents aren't the leading cause of death in Taiwan, I can't imagine why not.

I'd chosen the United Hotel for a variety of reasons—because it was affordable but not scary cheap (I wasn't about to end up in the

Taiwanese equivalent of the Tampa La Quinta), because it was right next to the subway, and because it had a semi-comprehensible English-language website, which promised "luxuriously decorated corridor poles." That sold me.

The United Hotel is, according to their website, on Kwang-Fu South Road, which it turns out is the same as GuangFu South Road. When Romanizing Chinese, two systems are in common use in Taiwan—Pinyin and Wade-Giles—which means that the district 中山區 can be written in English as either Zhongshan or Chung-shan, depending on which guidebook you use or which street sign you choose to believe. I don't know whose fault this ridiculous system is, but I've decided to blame the British, just because Wade-Giles sounds so poncey. To make things even more interesting, both of these Romanizations can also be very easily mispronounced by a non-Chinese-speaker, so I found it best to just point to the map when taking a taxi, lest I wind up in the Zongzheng (or Chung-cheng) district instead of Zhongshan (or Chung-shan) . . . or something like that. Frankly, I'm still confused.

The Yankees were on a tear when I arrived in Taipei in August 2007, clawing their way up from a huge deficit to within four games of the first-place Red Sox, and in a virtual tie for the wild card. They looked like they'd been revitalized by their farm system, bringing up players like the affably manic power hitter Shelley Duncan and pitching phenom Joba Chamberlain, who had an all-time classic athlete sob story (Native American, raised by a poor single father half paralyzed with polio who played catch with his son from a wheelchair) and a beautiful slider.

The fans in Taipei knew all that, and then some. The two questions I was asked most often were "Why did America reelect George Bush?" and "Why is Kyle Farnsworth still on the team?" neither of which I could answer to anyone's satisfaction.

Near midnight on one of my first nights in the city, I left my hotel to head down the block to the 7-Eleven. I defend my fixation with Taiwanese convenience stores by arguing that you can tell a lot about a culture by its 7-Elevens. Really, though, I was just fascinated by the strange foods (asparagus juice) and packaging. It's sort of nice to be free of the ability to read label information, and the accompanying responsibility; I was transformed into a marketer's ideal consumer, making my decisions solely on images, design, and placement. I didn't know how many calories or grams of fat or vitamins were in anything I ate; sometimes I didn't even know what the main ingredient was.

It was raining and windy, so I dug the Yankees umbrella I'd brought to give to an email contact out of my suitcase and headed out. "Be careful. There's a typhoon," said the woman at the front desk as I passed—much to my surprise. True, I had seen a little hurricane-shaped icon on the news, but, not knowing whether it referred to past, present, or future events, or meant something else entirely, I'd shrugged it off. (To be honest, I'm not sure what exactly distinguished this "typhoon" from a slightly worse than usual rainstorm, but technically there *were* two typhoons while I was in Taiwan, and since that sounds dramatic and exciting, I may as well make the most of them.)

At the 7-Eleven I picked up the aforementioned asparagus juice, wasabi peas, some sort of yogurt and cereal kit, and a mystery product that later turned out to be, I think, green tea bean paste cookies. Maybe. As I was paying the clerk, a thin guy in his early twenties with long straggly hair nodded at my Yankeees umbrella and said in thickly accented but excellent English: "You know they designated Mike Myers for assignment today?"

Baseball came to Taiwan via the occupying Japanese in the early twentieth century, the Japanese having been introduced to the game decades before by an American professor at Tokyo University. As I learned from *Playing in Isolation*, where I got almost all of this history, because of Taiwan's long tradition of Confucianism—which prized studying and academic achievement while denigrating athletic activity as subservient and a waste of time—many Taiwanese were outright hostile to the game when it was first introduced. I wish I'd known about this line of thought in high school gym class. Anyway, baseball gradually gained popularity, for complex reasons of cultural identity and also because it is awesome, and it really took off in the seventies amidst nationalistic fervor, when Taiwan started kicking ass in the Little League World Series. (As documented in Yu's book, this involved years of all-consuming, near-abusive practices as well as extensive district gerrymandering, but never mind.)

Taiwan has its own pro league, the Chinese Professional Baseball League (CPBL), but it's nowhere near as popular as the U.S. game; just as it was starting to find some success, in the late nineties, it was rocked by a series of hair-raising gambling and corruption scandals that make the 1919 Chicago Black Sox look like church bingo. Players were kidnapped, pistol-whipped, and pressured to throw games; a coach was stabbed walking home from a match; the China Times Eagles had all but two of their Taiwanese players arrested, indicted, or implicated midseason and had to borrow personnel from other teams just to finish out the schedule.

As you might imagine, these incidents dampened the CPBL's popularity and attendance numbers considerably. But in recent years, the arrival of Wang and a few other Taiwanese players in America has hastened the decline. That spiked a huge interest in Major League Baseball and led to far more U.S. games on television. The significant gap in the level of play between the CPBL and MLB has only widened, with promising Taiwanese players now signing abroad. As one fan at a CPBL game told me, "After watching American baseball, this is like watching kids play."

For a country with (one can only assume, given the history of the Chinese Professional Baseball League) a not-insignificant organized crime problem, Taiwan feels remarkably safe. Walking down pitch-black alleys at midnight in foreign countries nine thousand miles from home is probably a bad idea as a rule, but it didn't *feel* dangerous—I didn't pick up any of the vibes that might worry me on an American city street, from the condition of the buildings to the body language of people I passed. Maybe I just didn't know what vibes to be on the lookout for. But I only worried that if anything *did* happen, I'd look like an utter moron: "So, Ms. Span, where did you lose your passport?" "Well, I was just walking down this strange unlit alley late at night . . ."

(In fact, I should have been afraid, but for a completely different reason: Taipei has the most enormous cockroaches I've ever seen. If you just caught a glimpse of one out of the corner of your eye you might think they were smallish iguanas. Travel tip: when walking at night, wear closed-toed shoes.)

Taiwan is twelve hours ahead of New York, which means a Tuesday night game on the East Coast will air live in Taiwan at seven Wednesday morning. Some people watch at home before work, but many wait for one of the reruns later that night. I'd been talking to a number of Taiwanese fans online and hoped to meet up with one or two to watch Chien-Ming Wang. But like just about everything else that year, Taiwan didn't go exactly as I'd planned: Chien-Ming Wang—or, as I kept forgetting to call him, Wang Chien-Ming—endured, while I was there, the worst start of his professional career. I had crossed the Pacific to watch him give up eight runs to the Blue Jays in less than three innings at seven-thirty in the morning and, not surprisingly, not many Taiwanese seemed to feel the need to relive the experience later that night. I went to several sports bars where the game was usually a big draw; they were sparsely populated with expats, mostly Brits and Australians watching soccer.

Wang did, however, make news that day for showing emotion: when he was removed from the game, he tossed his glove into the dugout in frustration, a typical enough American reaction to that kind of start but very rare in Taiwanese athletics. I was hesitant to write about this because it seems dangerously close to endorsing some kind of stoic-Asian stereotype, but then I heard so many Taiwanese people themselves mention it—there were actual headlines because the man threw his glove down, and not just in the sports section— that I guess if it's a stereotype, it's one a lot of Taiwanese have embraced. Later that week Junwei Yu's friend told me that the open emotions were one of the main reasons he preferred American baseball; he wanted to watch players react.

Wang himself is a bit of an enigma in Taiwan, and more of one in the States. He's quiet and soft-spoken with reporters, a quality at first attributed to his lack of English. Wang chose not to use a translator in America, going for the full immersion experience and picking up the language from his teammates and, he said, movies and television. He speaks English pretty well these days, but he's still publicly a man of few words. He tends to answer questions politely but in as few words as possible. He jokes around with teammates and coaches, but mostly in private.

Once I arrived in Taiwan, I wondered how much of his reserve came naturally and how much might be the result of being extraordinarily scrutinized in Taiwan. He's a bigger star there than Derek Jeter is in the States. Wang had seemingly infinite endorsements—food, clothing, cars, computers, you name it—and his every pitch and night out were deconstructed in the papers and on the news. When he flew home after his first season in the majors, there was such a mob waiting outside his house that he and his wife were trapped in their car for an hour and the police had to be called.

In Taichung, south of Taipei, I met Howard Lin, the man who'd selected a young Wang for the Taiwanese national team and coached him for a year and a half. He told me that he didn't think Wang's reserve was a result of the language barrier, that the pitcher had been quiet as long as he'd known him. "But," he added through a translator, "he has a heart of metal." I couldn't determine if he meant steel or gold, but either way it was clearly intended as a compliment.

I'd gone to Taichung to meet Junwei Yu, author of *Playing in Isolation*, who taught at the physical education college there. The city is several hours south of Taipei by train, past mountains and rice paddies. I didn't see any other westerners as I spent several hours walking around, though I did see plenty of Yankee logos, on mopeds and helmets, backpacks and caps. No one at the train station spoke English, and I felt like the typical arrogant American tourist, bumbling around without speaking ten words of the local language but counting on the locals to know mine. I ended up having to give Yu's phone number to the nice woman at the information desk so that he could tell her where I was going and have her write down the address in Chinese characters so I could show a taxi driver.

Yu was a little younger than I expected. Unlike most of his compatriots, he's not a Yankees fan—instead he roots for the Houston Astros because when he was a boy he happened to catch a TV broadcast of Game 1 of the 1986 NLCS, the one where Mike Scott completely dominated the Mets. Every MLB team has at least a few Taiwanese fans—someone who studied in Montreal might now be a Nationals fan, and so on—and they're starting to resent the Yankees now, just like most Americans. I consider this a sign of the sport's healthy growth.

As I was drinking green tea with Yu and Howard Lin and a few other faculty members, Chang Tai-Shan, the slugging third baseman of the CPBL's Sinon Bulls, walked in with zero fanfare, poured himself some tea, and started chatting with the group. The Bulls had a game that night at the university, and he'd come in to say hello and pass the time. This isn't something you'll see Alex Rodriguez doing anytime soon, and more than anything else it brought home to me the stark difference in magnitude between baseball stardom there and in the States.

Chang shared, with Yu translating, some of his thoughts on what the CPBL had to do to improve ("First, you have to be handsome"). He talked about the need for better facilities and marketing, creating a real farm system, and, most of all, improving the level of play. There's no free agency in the CPBL, meaning players can't choose for themselves whom to play for, and salaries are kept down; efforts to unionize have repeatedly been stamped out by the owners. Chang noted that it took nearly a hundred years of baseball for free agency to arrive in the States, so maybe Taiwan had another eighty to go. It was an interesting antidote to all the endless American baseball complaints about inflated salaries and mercenary players.

Back in Taipei, I tried to soak up as many sights as I could. I went to the top of the vertiginous Taipei 101 building, saw the Sun Yat-Sen Memorial, and most of all went to the night markets, which were mostly tourist traps—the same faux-jade carvings for sale at stall after stall—but still such a mesmerizing, frenzied sensory overload that it was well worth battling the crowds and buying a couple of over-priced mementos. For the first time in my life I sort of understood why someone would voluntarily go to Times Square.

Still, it was hard to feel comfortable—I didn't know where I was going, I didn't speak the language, and I didn't have as precise an idea as I might have liked of why exactly I had flown myself halfway around the world and what I was supposed to do now. So, as usual, I retreated into baseball.

I remember those Yankees games unusually clearly, compared to the long summer string that usually blurs together. Joba Chamberlain made his debut in one, and another featured a near-brawl with the Toronto Blue Jays because somebody plunked A-Rod (in perceived re-taliation, as I recall, for the play a few weeks earlier when he yelled "Ha!" to distract a Jays fielder from a pop-up). I watched these games on the hotel TV, with ebullient Chinese announcers talking over the faint sound of the Americans in the YES booth. I couldn't understand anything except the occasional name or "Home run!"

After I got home, a helpful reader online pointed out that I could have pushed a single button on the hotel TV and listened to the Amer-ican game broadcast. But I'm actually sort of glad I didn't know that.

The night after my trip to Taichung, Junwei and his friend took me to see the Brother Elephants play the Sinon Bulls in a stadium on the northern fringe of Taipei. They were good-natured about the trip, but had an air I recognized immediately as almost identical to that of New Yorkers shepherding out-of-town friends or family to the Rockefeller Center tree lighting or the Empire State Building. Neither of them had been to a CPBL game in years.

There were probably fewer than two thousand people in attendance, a minor-league-sized crowd. The stadium felt that way, too, due for a renovation in the way of many minor-league parks, and with a view of steep mountains beyond the outfield fences.

It's always the small differences that obsess me in situations like these. Players chewed watermelon seeds instead of sunflower seeds. The pitch velocity was of course shown in kilometers per hour, so that a changeup's speed appeared on the scoreboard as "128." Each team's supporters sat completely segregated on opposite sides of the stands, like at British soccer games, and both teams had a spirited group of mixed-gender cheerleaders who waved huge flags, chanted, and pounded on drums every time their team was batting. Junwei pointed out that the incessant drums probably weren't helping the CPBL attendance figures any.

Snippets of American songs played during the game—"She'll Be Comin' Around the Mountain," "The Battle Hymn of the Republic," and for some reason "Popeye the Sailor Man." My first impulse was to call these choices random, but upon reflection, I don't suppose they're any odder than the Mets' "Lazy Mary" or the Yankees' hackneyed "Cotton-Eyed Joe" routine.

A few foreign players were on every CPBL team, most former MLB fringe players or prospects who'd washed out of the system. Robinson Cano's father, Jose, spent several years playing in Taiwan in the 1990s and was, I'm told, hugely popular there. I didn't recognize any of the Western players on the Bulls or the Brother Elephants, but I had noted several familiar faces in a CPBL game I'd watched on TV earlier in the week—Pete Munro, a former Astro and Blue Jay with a career 4.88 ERA in the majors, and Wayne Franklin, very briefly a Yankee reliever back in 2005, now a Uni-President Lion.

I felt a thrill of undeserved pride at the popularity of American baseball in Taiwan—here was *something* we could still do right. The success does seem to have come at the expense of local tradition, which is why the Taiwanese won't get to see players like Chien-Ming Wang pitch at home, or why the Sinon Bulls struggle to draw fans while Yankees games are repeated on TV four times daily. Globalization at its best and worst, I suppose. The impact (and, more cynically, marketing opportunities) of the Yankees on this island, which is literally half a world away and not even recognized as a country by the American government, is impressive. The morning after walking by snack stands selling chicken feet and listening to Mandarin cheers at the Bulls–Elephants game, I sat cross-legged on the floor of my hotel room, surrounded by "luxuriously decorated corridor poles," and watched the Yankees beat the Indians.

CHAPTER 10

Rhubarb and Wonderboy

My movie obsession predates my baseball obsession by a considerable length of time. As soon as I was old enough to sit up for two hours, my parents took me to a movie just about every week, without much regard to genre, quality, or—especially when I went with my dad—age-appropriateness. (*Terminator 2* at age nine stands out for me, not just for the memorable scenes of nuclear apocalypse but because I had my eyes closed for so much of the film that I missed half the plot, and we had to go back and see it again the next week.)

Between going to the theater, TV, renting, and Netflixing, it's a toss-up whether I've seen more movies or more baseball games in my life, but the count on both has to be in the thousands, which probably explains why I haven't cured cancer yet. So it makes sense that I've got a particular fascination with baseball movies. What makes less sense is why there are so few good ones.

I hate *The Natural*. *Field of Dreams* is better, but not my cup of tea. Going much farther back, *Take Me Out to the Ballgame* is far suckier than any movie involving Gene Kelly, Frank Sinatra, and ballplayers should ever be, and *Pride of the Yankees* has aged worse than Mo Vaughn. There is a handful of very good baseball films, mostly comedies—*Bull Durham* being my favorite, and *Major League*, and *Bad News Bears*—and some decent serious ones: *Eight Men Out, Bang the Drum Slowly, A League of Their Own*. But there aren't many of them, really, and I don't think there's ever been a truly *great* movie made about baseball. You'd think two classic American pastimes would go better together—consider how many great movies there are about organized crime, or for that matter, how many great movies there are about movies. What's so uncinematic about baseball?

The Natural, which manages to keep all the pompous grandiosity of its source material but none of its integrity, and which is at least forty-five minutes longer than it needs to be no matter how pretty Robert Redford is, has to be on my list of the most overrated movies of all time. I may be overreacting. When I'm not crazy about a movie that everyone else seems to love, sometimes I start to actively hate it in reaction; this happened with *Amelie,* a well-made sappy quirkfest about a pathologically charming French girl, which got so many raves from critics and friends that my casual dislike turned into unjustified white-hot loathing. (See also *Life Is Beautiful.*) But although *The Natural* may be better in many ways than your average Hollywood cheese, it's also vastly more pretentious. I usually prefer a silly movie that knows what it is to self-serious Oscar bait that overestimates its own intelligence. (See also *Crash.*)

You probably know the story already, but to review: Young and supertalented ballplayer Roy Hobbs (Redford in gauzy lighting, doing his best to play nineteen at forty-seven) comes up to the majors in the 1920s, only to be seduced, shot, and nearly killed by a mysterious woman, his career cut short before he even gets in a game. Years later, now middle-aged, Hobbs reemerges, joins the New York Knights, and leads the team all the way to the edge of a pennant, despite the corrupt machinations of their owner, "the Judge." Glenn Close plays the nice woman who loves him, but Roy loves Kim Basinger instead, even though she's a plant from the Judge and is negatively affecting his performance on the field—you know how women are. Oh, and he also has a magic bat named Wonderboy. (Lame name for a magic bat, if you ask me; sounds more like what

Jose Canseco might have nicknamed his penis.) But in the end he doesn't need the magic bat to rise off his sickbed and hit a dramatic game-winning homer to give the Knights the pennant. In the famous climactic scene, which you've no doubt seen before, the ball hits the stadium lights and they explode in a shower of sparks as Redford rounds the bases in super-duper slo-mo and inspirational music swells. Finally he marries the good girl, moves back to the wholesome countryside, and plays some catch with his son.

The Natural was directed by Barry Levinson, who was then still at the top of the decades-long downward spiral that would take him from *Diner* to *Envy* (which is about jealousy . . . and also a spray that makes dog shit disappear), so I'm not sure how things went so wrong. It's not so much that *The Natural* is long and humorless, or that Robert Redford appears to have somnambulated through several crucial weeks of filming, or that it's got an over-the-top virgin/whore complex, although all those are issues. No, the real problem is that I read the Bernard Malamud book first. And I didn't even *like* the book—it's a morality tale, a mannered, dry take on Arthurian legend. But if you read it and then watch the end of the movie . . . I don't want to ruin anything, but let's just say that in the book Roy Hobbs doesn't hit a home run and live happily ever after. At all.

In fact—and on second thought, I'm gonna go ahead and ruin it—at the end of the book Hobbs strikes out; the Knights lose the game; he tries to return the Judge's bribe money, but it's too late; everyone realizes the fix was on; his reputation and career are ruined; he's maimed the one woman who really loves him, Iris, with a foul ball; and the woman *he* loves tries to shoot him. It's a story of failure, doom, weakness, and disgrace that makes Dostoyevsky's more downbeat works seem like *Jonathan Livingston Seagull*. Last line: " . . . he lifted his hands to his face and wept many bitter tears."

So. Then you watch the last scenes of the movie, and as people around you are tearing up at the beautiful imagery and soaring music while Redford circles the bases in slow motion, all you can think is:

You have got to be fucking kidding me. It has to be one of the more cynical betrayals of source material ever put to film, the equivalent of ending a *Hamlet* adaptation with a lovely wedding between the prince and Ophelia.

The Natural is, in my opinion, far sappier and duller than *Field of Dreams,* which at least has a sense of humor and was clearly made by people who genuinely adore baseball. Unlike with *The Natural,* if you held a mirror up to this movie's face, it would fog up. But both movies share an obsession with father-son games of catch and are, I would have to say, the male equivalent of chick flicks—I just may not be the target audience. I vaguely remember playing catch with my dad a few times growing up, and I'm sure it was a lovely experience. But for film heroes it's become trite shorthand for paternal love.

I was disappointed by another supposed classic, too, as *Pride of the Yankees* has not aged well at all. It has its moments, and I love both Lou Gehrig and Gary Cooper (and Walter Brennan, and Babe Ruth playing himself) enough that I can't quite trash it. But I probably should, because there's actually a scene in which Gehrig visits Billy, "a little crippled kid," in the hospital, and promises to hit not one but two home runs for him if the kid promises to try to get better, because "there isn't anything you can't do if you try hard enough." And hit two homers he does, the second coming in his last at-bat, of course. Years later when Gehrig himself has gotten sick and is shuffling into Yankee Stadium for his farewell speech, little Billy is there waiting for him, all grown up. Billy's been standing there all day because he just had to tell Mr. Gehrig: "I did what you said. I tried hard, and I made it! Look, I can walk!" Look, I can roll my eyes so violently they hit my back teeth!

Over the years I've gone to considerable lengths looking for a great forgotten baseball movie. And I haven't found it, not yet—but I have found some incredibly weird ones. Which is almost as good.

I can't remember exactly when I developed a passion for watching bad movies—not mediocre movies, like *The Natural,* but absolute messes like the immortal Ed Wood classic *Plan 9 from Outer Space* or the mind-blowing *Troll 2* (which doesn't even reference the first *Troll,* is actually about goblins, and has the moral "Do not vacation in a town whose name is *goblin* spelled backward, especially not if the ghost of your dead grandfather has warned you against it.").

I suspect I picked up my love of terrible acting, creaky plots, and subpar visuals from a proud family tradition, starting when I was about twelve, of gathering around to watch *Walker: Texas Ranger* together. In case you've not been lucky enough to catch it, it's a hilariously tone-deaf show (from its Chuck Norris–sung opening credits: "For the eyes of a Ranger are upon you, anything you do he's gonna see / When you're in Texas look behind you, 'cause that's where the Ranger's gonna be"), full of ham-handed, earnest anti-drug and -gang rhetoric, and with a touching faith in the ability of children's karate classes to solve any and all social problems. It was also so comfortingly predictable that we used to have running bets on who could most accurately predict the entire episode plot from the first few minutes: "That guy with the European accent is obviously evil—I mean, he's named Broussard, come on—and he's going to kidnap Alex [Walker's long-suffering and oft-kidnapped love interest] after the third commercial break and hold her at the ranch!" It's my first memory of deliberately watching something terrible and enjoying it specifically for its badness.

But certainly not my last. Finding a really great obscure awful movie—like *WaxWork,* which came on TV around 3:00 a.m. one glorious night my junior year of college—is still a moment of triumph for me. It's only recently that I've discovered the fascinating world of Sci-Fi Channel movies (now SyFy, which is even better) but it turns out I'm just not capable of channel-surfing past something called, say, *Kraken: Tentacles of the Deep* or *Gargoyles: Wings of Darkness* or the one that started it all, *Bats: Human Harvest.* Typically these are filmed in Eastern Europe on what looks to be a budget of five grand and star pretty, wooden actors whom you may recognize from a Kmart ad or a long-defunct nineties genre show, with CGI that could be topped by a half-clever twelve-year-old. I love these movies.

I was in the Hall of Fame one day, in the middle of a cold February with several feet of snow blanketing Cooperstown, working on an article for the *Voice,* when I wandered through their baseball movie display. It's not the most spectacular part of the Hall, mostly props and posters, but one of those posters caught my eye: *Rhubarb—The Millionaire Tom Cat.* It's a great title, the kind you can't just let pass, at least not if you're me. It's about what happens when an eccentric millionaire leaves his struggling baseball team, the Brooklyn Loons, to a cat. It stars Ray Milland and a cat. "The funniest picture in nine lifetimes," crows one of its taglines, though I imagine that's only true if you spent those nine lifetimes in Communist Russia.

This movie (which, stunningly enough, is not available on DVD) became something of an obsession of mine, and so eventually I tracked it down and ordered the VHS tape. I knew there was a reason I hadn't thrown out my VCR.

You might recall Ray Milland from his heartbreaking performance in *The Lost Weekend,* for which he won an Academy Award. And you might recall Orangey the cat from his performance as "Cat" in *Breakfast at Tiffany's,* for which he won a Patsy Award—the animal equivalent of the Oscars, given out between 1951 and 1984 but now tragically defunct. (The very first Patsy was given to Francis, the mule from *Francis the Talking Mule.* Also, Orangey was trained by Frank Inn, who also worked with Patsy Award winner Arnold the Pig on *Green Acres.* Now you know. You're welcome.)

Naturally, in *Rhubarb,* the Brooklyn Loons start winning when Rhubarb takes over, and the players become superstitious about it (this movie depicts ballplayers as having the intellect of slow second graders), which means their chance at the pennant is put in jeopardy when Rhubarb gets catnapped, because without the cat the team's confidence is shot. More detail is probably not necessary, except to say that the hero's fiancée's severe allergy to Rhubarb is a major plot point and apparently admissible in court as evidence of identity.

Rhubarb turned out to be stilted, silly, and just plain odd enough to be entertaining, but it was not actively terrible. For that I recommend a movie called *Night Game,* which I read about on an extremely comprehensive list of baseball movies, and knew immediately that I needed to see.

Another film inexplicably passed over by DVD distributors, *Night Game* stars Roy Scheider as a Houston police detective in the eighties (very, *very* much in the eighties). I saw *Jaws* at a very young and impressionable age; for years I would nervously check for fins even in the deep end of a swimming pool at the Y, and even now I tend to anxiously scan the horizon when in the ocean. So I have a soft spot for Scheider and would like to point out that it really isn't his fault the movie is so awful. Listen to the plot and tell me if even Laurence Olivier could have done anything with this:

There's a serial killer on the loose, and he's killing blond women with a hook in what turns out to be a pattern—one murder every time a certain Houston Astros pitcher wins a night game at home. Scheider's character, who is presented as a likeable, straight-shooting kind of guy even though he is dating his ex-girlfriend's daughter, is on the case. This is the kind of movie where a scantily clad blonde, when being chased by a vicious hook-handed murderer, will not only run away from all the people and lights of a carnival onto a dark, empty beach but then actually run up the stairs of a desolate construction project, thus trapping herself completely alone.

Anyway, toward the end, Scheider makes a blood-chilling discovery (spoiler alert!): a Houston Astros pitcher got cut from spring training a while back and then, as he was dejectedly leaving the complex, was hit by a bus, a tragic accident in which he lost his hand. And now whenever his replacement wins a home night game he goes out and kills a blond woman. We've all been there, right? I mean, every time the guy who replaced me at the *Voice* gets a cover story, I go out and strangle a pigeon.

_____

I actually had some expectations for 1962's *Safe at Home,* which stars (sort of) Mickey Mantle and Roger Maris, in the flesh, with cameos from then-manager Ralph Houk and Whitey Ford. Now that I think about it, *Safe at Home* would make a much better scary-serial-killer title than *Night Game.* But instead it's about a nine-year-old named Hutch who tries to impress his Little League teammates by claiming he and his father are friends with Mickey Mantle and Roger Maris, then runs away to spring training to try to convince the Yankee superstars to attend his team's awards banquet. Hijinks ensue, sort of, and everyone runs around yelling, "Gosh! Gee!"

I discovered the existence of *Safe at Home* just by accident a year or two ago, when I was, for reasons that now completely elude me, searching for information on Joe Pepitone. In an old "Sports of the Times" story, I came across an Arthur Daley account of lighthearted batting-cage banter regarding Mantle and Maris's upcoming movie premiere, and did a double-take. Mantle and Maris starred in a movie? How come I'd never heard of it?

Well, that question turned out to have an easy answer: because it's really, really bad. Even *The Natural* is a much better movie than *Safe at Home,* in part because it turns out that Wonderboy is able to convey a far wider range of emotions on film than Mickey Mantle. It seems mean-spirited to rag too much on the acting in this movie: the kids are, after all, just kids, while Mantle and Maris and manager Ralph Houk are amateurs. But the end result is that only one of the movie's main characters is actually played by a capable actor, and the whole thing resembles nothing so much as an eighty-four-minute version of an old Post cereal ad.

Hutch has recently moved from New York to Florida with his father, who owns a charter fishing boat. Hutch cooks, cleans, and takes care of his father's laundry, which was almost enough to make me want children, but it's made clear that in fact we're supposed to think Hutch's dad is putting too much adult responsibility on him. And in a subplot never seen on the big screen before or since, he's missing his son's Little League games because of work! When a bully starts giving Hutch crap about his father, he spins his lie about Mantle and Maris, and it spirals out of control, as these things always do in movies (but not in real life, where one of my middle school classmates successfully convinced everyone for years that her uncle had murdered Jimmy Hoffa and buried him under Lot D at the Meadowlands). So Hutch sets out for Fort Lauderdale to meet Mantle and Maris and enlist their help.

The movie came out in 1962, but its heart is completely in the fifties. It takes place in a world in which every single human being is cheerful and friendly (even the bully is fairly polite) and crime is nonexistent; nothing this idyllic ever shows up on movie screens these days except at the beginning of horror films. Anyway, eventually Mantle and Maris take a liking to Hutch, and they're really perfectly likeable on-screen, but they appear to have seen their lines for the first time five minutes before filming began. The kid also endears himself to the obligatory crusty old coach—William "Fred Mertz" Frawley, the lone capable actor mentioned above. Meanwhile, Whitey Ford's advertised cameo consists of just one completely expressionless sentence ("Houk wants to see you right away"). They should've gotten Yogi.

Eventually Hutch explains his situation to Mantle and Maris. Though they have no other plans, they refuse to come to the banquet, because Lying Is Wrong. After a stern and decidedly judgmental lecture—"You can't make a foul ball fair by moving the baseline. It's just not in the rules!"—that leaves Hutch near tears, the kid agrees to tell his teammates the truth, just as his dad shows up to comfort him. (And if I were a hardworking widower fishing boat captain, I'm not sure I would take as kindly as Hutch's dad does to parenting tips from the Mick, but never mind.)

However, after Hutch makes his painful public confession to his teammates, his father declares that Hutch now has two new friends—and they've invited the whole Little League team down to meet the Yankees and watch spring training. Everyone is thrilled, Hutch is a hero, and I try to remember why it was again, exactly, that lying was supposed to be bad and harmful, instead of totally awesome. (It reminds me of the way *The Wizard of Oz* tries to pretend that its lesson is "If I ever go looking for my heart's desire again, I won't look any further than my own backyard. Because if it isn't there, I never really lost it to begin with!" Not only does that make no sense when you break it down, but in fact, every frame of the movie is screaming at you to get the hell off the family farm, run away to a big city, and hang out with weirdos and misfits. Has a kid ever watched it and said, "Gee, I better not go off and have any adventures"? Least sincere moral ever.)

So why aren't there more good baseball movies? I suppose there aren't a ton of truly great sports movies, period—a few here and there, but it's not been exactly the most creatively fertile genre. Still, I feel that, given its impressive literary tradition (Thomas Boswell wrote that more good baseball books appear in a single year than have been written about football in the past fifty years, which may be an exaggeration but not a big one), there ought to be plenty of great baseball films yet to be made. Maybe it's that it's hard to balance the tone, going for either the bawdy locker-room comedy or the self-serious "America's pastime" approach. Maybe studios think the average sports fan isn't smart enough to want really thoughtful and intelligent baseball flicks.

In the end, it probably doesn't matter all that much, because baseball can tell its own stories. The Tampa Bay Rays going from last place to first in 2008 wasn't much less believable than the hapless Indians doing the same in *Major League*, and the 2004 Red Sox World Series could have easily been a movie plot, although it might not seem believable enough; in fact, when it was grafted onto the romantic comedy plot of *Fever Pitch*, it felt to me like a cheesy movie cliché even though it had just happened. Unadapted baseball is full of drama and plots.

Still, tragically few of those plots involve hook-handed pitchers going on killing sprees, or team-owning cats (or, in a movie I'd pay a heck of a lot to see, both). That's why we still need Hollywood.

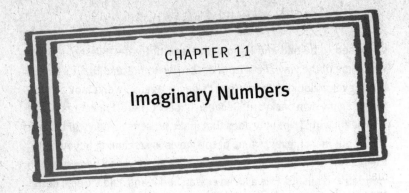

I often wish I liked math more, because I hate playing into the stereotype of the girl who, gosh, just doesn't have a head for numbers. And really, it's not that I was ever bad at math so much as I merely loathed it. I enjoy baseball stats both old and new, but I prefer the new ones, more because they drive the grouchy old men of the baseball establishment insane than because I have any particularly clear idea of the calculations that go into WARP2.* I have a ton of respect for mathematics, in theory. In practice I've always preferred subjects in which I could, if necessary, bullshit my way through.

I still remember the moment when math lost me: ninth or tenth grade, algebra, when we began a segment in class on imaginary numbers. An imaginary number, you might or might not recall, is the square root of a negative number; they use i to signify the square root of -1. (I don't even know who I mean by "they" in the previous sentence—the shadowy international conspiracy responsible for algebra? Rafael Bombelli, Descartes, and their sinister henchmen?)

Now, you might say there is no such thing as a square root of a

---

*The same as WARP, only it also takes league difficulty into account. WARP is Wins Above Replacement Player, which per the mad scientists at Baseball Prospectus is "the number of wins this player contributed, above what a replacement level hitter, fielder, and pitcher would have done, with adjustments only for within the season." I like this stat, which is very useful for comparing players' offense, but I would have to go back to school for several years if I wanted to be able to figure out how they came up with the formula behind it.

negative number, because a negative integer times a negative integer is a positive integer, and you would be right. This is why they had to invent an imaginary one.

If I'm not explaining this well, it's probably because it makes no sense at all. Basically, as I understand it, a bunch of mathematicians decided it would be helpful if they could calculate the square root of negative numbers—and rather than accept the fact that you can't actually do that, they just started making stuff up. I can certainly respect that, one bullshitter to another, but I was damned if I was going to go along and pretend I had the foggiest idea what they were talking about. I could plug in the appropriate formula for the test, but I never got the underlying concepts on a gut level, and after *i*, I was just going through the motions. As soon as I was allowed to, I dropped math like a hot coal. I never got to precalc, let alone calc, and by the time I realized, halfway through college, that this may have been an unwise decision, it was too late to catch up. So instead I fulfilled my science and math requirements with classes like Science Fiction, Science Fact, in which much of my grade was based on a short-story assignment. I wrote mine about mutants, drawing on half-remembered concepts from *The X-Men*.

So now, much the way I sometimes wish I were a doctor or scientist, in a field with objectively correct processes and facts and provable conclusions, I can only wish I were a better stathead. Stat geeks are my people, basically, or should be, but I can't contribute much to the conversation. I'm not totally hopeless—I know what VORP* is, and what a VORP of 45 means (Albert Pujols) and what a VORP of -8.3 means (Sidney Ponson), but the actual formula that determines VORP remains as comprehensible to me as a Sanskrit edition of *Ulysses*.

---

*Value Over Replacement Player. Baseball Prospectus again: "The number of runs contributed beyond what a replacement-level player at the same position would contribute if given the same percentage of team plate appearances." A replacement player is the kind of player a team could get at minimal cost, for example, from the minors, who plays at "replacement level," significantly worse than the average major leaguer. People like to make fun of this one, I think mostly because VORP is a silly-sounding acronym, but it's pretty awesome.

You don't need to get that part of it, though, to appreciate these numbers and what people have done with them—just like I can see that the equation $e^{i\pi} + 1 = 0$ is pretty awesome, even though I can't fully grasp what it means. I don't have a mind for that, or at least, I never cared enough to train my mind to work that way. In the meantime, I take it on faith that the Baseball Prospectus guys know their stuff—and they do. But there will always be something a little inorganic for me in using these statistics, a necessary mental translation into older stats, an extra step. I can calculate batting average by myself just sitting in the stands, but not EqERA.

Perhaps that's why some sportswriters are so virulently resistant to new statistics—not just uninterested but actively offended. Maybe they're like I was when first exposed to imaginary numbers: you know the concept makes sense to a small group of smart people somewhere, but you don't get it on a gut level, and it ticks you off enough that you don't even want to try. It feels like they're just making stuff up.

To complicate matters, the sabermetrics/*Moneyball*-versus-scouting/instinct argument has gotten all mixed up with the blog-versus-newspaper argument, creating one giant generation-gap catfight. And so it became the fashion for mainstream sportswriters to be dismissive not just of advanced statistics but also of anyone who uses them, and then of anyone who writes primarily for the Internet. Despite the fact that almost every beat writer and regular baseball reporter in the country is now forced to do some sort of blogging, a surprising number of them still talk with naked contempt about those online losers who seem to think they know so much. Bill Conlin, a venerable Philadelphia sportswriter, made waves online several years back when he told a blogger who had emailed to criticize his MVP vote for Jimmy Rollins: "The only positive thing I can think of about Hitler's time on earth—I'm sure he would have eliminated all bloggers."

It's a two-way street, and many sports bloggers have taken up a deep and abiding distaste for mainstream reporters as well. Nearly every popular sports blog features regular criticism of the mainstream sports media—some of it thoroughly justified, some of it not. Sometimes a well-reasoned and thoughtful critique is undercut by its commenters, who in the way of anonymous trolls everywhere can get viciously personal with very little provocation.

The dispute is ultimately a silly one, since nobody cares much about this epic battle besides the actual media members and bloggers themselves. That includes me twice over, from both sides of the aisle, so I find the catfight pretty hypnotic. But there's not much logic at play here. Blogs are just a means of communicating information, like radio or newspapers or television, without implying inherently superior or inferior writing or reseach. And they aren't going anywhere, so you might as well rail against the horseless carriage. On the other side, beat writers still serve an important function—yes, we can watch every game for ourselves now, and no, players almost never say anything interesting these days, but you still need someone in there to ask them, just in case, and to convey a sense of their personalities and demeanor.

Beat writers are not paid for their blogs, despite all the work that goes into them; perhaps it's not surprising that dealing with a handful of moronic commenters on the blogs they were forced to write for free was enough to launch some of them into comprehensive rants against the entire medium. It's a false dichotomy, though, especially when there's a nearly unquenchable interest in baseball and plenty of room for both. The newspaper industry may be in its death throes, but there's still plenty of interest in sports coverage, and it will persevere in one format or another. Or so I keep telling myself.

Columnists might be more justified in feeling a bit threatened by bloggers, since they tend to focus more on opinions, which, as the saying goes, are like assholes: everybody's got one. Murray Chass embodied the extreme edge of calcified antitechnology opinion in a column a few years ago. He was an excellent columnist at one point, or so I've been told, but he's come to symbolize a crusty refusal to either change with the times or respect anyone who does, as epitomized in a petulant rant about Baseball Prospectus and their statistical bent:

> To me, VORP epitomized the new-age nonsense. For the longest time, I had no idea what VORP meant and didn't care enough to go to any great lengths to find out. I asked some colleagues whose work I respect, and they didn't know what it meant either.
>
> Finally, not long ago, I came across VORP spelled out. It stands for value over replacement player. How thrilling. How absurd. Value over replacement player. Don't ask what it means. I don't know.

It's fine, obviously, if you don't like the newer statistics. You don't need them to write a great column. Red Smith did just fine without them, as did Roger Angell, and though I'd like to think that in their younger days both would have shown enough curiosity to look into the matter, maybe they wouldn't have. In any case, there are infinite ways to enjoy baseball, and none of them is objectively right or wrong as far as I'm concerned, except maybe leaving before the end of the game with your team down by four runs or less. Still, I believe one ought to find out what something means before trashing it in the *New York Times*—and in the case of VORP, the only "great length" you need to go to in order to do so is a three-second Google search and a few minutes on BaseballProspectus.com.

In the years since that column, Chass has left the *Times* and started his own blog—which he refuses to call a blog, insisting that it's instead "a site for baseball columns."

The baseball argument that you might call stats-versus-scouts—the *Moneyball* wars—is as much of a false dichotomy as blogs-versus-newspapers. I'm not sure why any sane person would agonize over choosing between advanced statistical analysis and reports by experienced scouts when in fact you can just use both.

So much ink has been spilled on *Moneyball* that it hardly seems worth rehashing the issue. But in brief, Michael Lewis wrote a book about the surprising success of the low-budget Oakland A's and how their GM, Billy Bean, was relying on unconventional strategies, advanced statistics, and genius types with no baseball background in order to exploit market inefficiencies and compete with much wealthier teams. *Moneyball* sounds like an unlikely bestseller, but Lewis is an engaging writer and he builds a compelling narrative around the 2002 draft. The book was a huge hit and accelerated baseball's move toward new methods of analysis, thoroughly pissing off the old guard in the process.

Leading the anti-*Moneyball* forces was Joe Morgan, who was once one of the greatest second basemen of all time and is now one of the least interesting baseball analysts on TV. Morgan steadfastly refused to read the book, which didn't stop him from asserting loudly and often it was "a joke," that "somebody who didn't play the game can't teach me about the game," and telling a *San Francisco Weekly* reporter back in 2005 that "I don't read books like that. I didn't read Bill James' book, and . . . he was complimenting me. Why would I wanna read a book about a computer, that gives computer numbers?" Told that it was not about computers, he replied, "Well, I'm not reading the book, so I wouldn't know." For some old-school players, managers, analysts, or reporters still clinging to a jocks-against-nerds mind-set, examining nonstandard statistical evidence has become a character flaw.

Take, for instance, a 2008 *New York Times* article about Billy Eppler, assistant to Brian Cashman and one of the Yankees' most influential scouts. Joe Torre's book painted an unflattering portrait of Eppler as someone without a real feel for the game, basically *accusing* him of being a stathead and therefore "ignoring the heartbeat of the game." In the article several people defend him against that charge—not because being statistically inclined wouldn't be a bad thing, but because they insist he actually doesn't know that much about stats.

Now, this guy was supposedly influential in the signings of Kyle

Farnsworth and Kei Igawa. So he probably doesn't. Still, it's an example of the frustrating anti-intellectual strain in baseball that rears its head every once in a while. Not that *Moneyball* is perfect, or that stats are the be-all and end-all; needless to say, as I'm someone whose only other interaction with numbers for the last decade has come when dividing restaurant bills, they're not what fascinate me most about the game. It's the stubborn, uncurious position that increased knowledge is somehow damaging baseball that drives me crazy. "The game is played by human beings, not by numbers!" is the anti-*Moneyball* rallying cry, as though anyone on earth were actually suggesting that anthropomorphized digits were out there on the field. Look, I don't understand math, either, but that's no reason to pretend it doesn't work, imaginary numbers and all.

With all that said, I do love the more human aspects of the game—watching players interact on the bench; seeing who's friends with whom, who seems like a decent guy, and whom I don't like; figuring out how a certain facet of personality might show itself in a guy's game, in his batting approach, or his baserunning. Paul O'Neill practicing his swing in the outfield, Turk Wendell's necklace of teeth and claws, Nomar Garciaparra's OCD fiddling in the batter's box—those details are what drew me to baseball in the first place, and they are still a large part of what keeps me coming back.

I read this quote from a George Plimpton article about the time he took the poet (and Dodgers fan) Marianne Moore to a World Series game at Yankee Stadium. He described what she told him about the way she first became a fan:

In the summer of 1949 she had been invited to Ebbets Field and saw Roy Campanella walk out to the mound to calm down a pitcher named Carl Spooner. He had stood there on the mound, resting the big catcher's mitt on his hip, the mask pushed back on the top of his head; and his earnest demeanor—his "zest," as she put it—something of that moment, and how he imparted his encouragement with a pat to Spooner's rump as the pitcher turned back to the mound, caught her fancy, indeed made a baseball addict of her.

I had a similar experience getting sucked into the game, albeit minus the rump patting as a big draw. So I'm the last person who would argue that baseball requires its fans to put more of an emphasis on numbers and less on personas.

But I can't have any illusions about it at this point in my life: an awful lot of this persona stuff is pretty much bullshit, and you can't always, or even often, find out much about a player just from watching him at the ballpark. I've long since made my peace with that. I'm not sure if it was one of baseball's many scandals or arrests that disillusioned me or if I was just never all that illusioned to begin with; I love watching baseball that way, but that particular aspect of it is no more real than a reality TV show. Humans are what interest me, but humans lie, and it's very hard to know what someone's truly like based on his on-field behavior, though it's fascinating to speculate.

Numbers lie, too, of course. But only because humans make them do it.

No, there's no wrong way to watch baseball, though I like some of them more than others. Many fans will argue that you can only truly root for one team, but if it brings someone pleasure to root for several different ball clubs, I don't see why that should bother me. And most die-hard fans have nothing but contempt for front-runners—anyone who starts getting into a team just as they're starting to get good, or who parachutes in for the playoffs and becomes a huge supporter just in time to watch them win it all. I understand the distaste, because it seems like that would cheapen the experience, a lazy shortcut to emotions that serious fans have been cultivating for years. But life is tough, and if a little front-running fair-weather fandom can bring some happiness into someone's day, who am I to say it's wrong? Even leaving a close game early makes sense if you have young kids with you, or important plans for the early morning, or . . . okay, fine, even if you want to beat the traffic, though I say that begrudgingly. The game should be there to make your life better, not tougher.

Baseball is entertainment and escapism, and while it can be more than that—inspiration, melodrama, elation, despair, morality play, tortured metaphor for anything you like—it doesn't have to be. And trying to force it rarely ends well. How many players have we been told are heroes and role models, and how many of those have turned out to have been drunks, gamblers, cheats, criminals, jerks? You can easily make baseball into something bigger than it is, but you do so at your own peril. And you can blame the players for failing to live up to your expectations, but after a certain point it's hard not to conclude that maybe it's time for you to adjust those expectations instead.

To me, that's the real message of the whole steroids mess—well, that and "shit rolls downhill," given the total lack of accountability by management, ownership, and Major League Baseball, but that's hardly news. When one baseball player is found to be using steroids, it's an outrage. When the 150th player is caught, it's hard for me to get too worked up. Faced with the probability that tons and tons of players were and still are using performance-enhancing drugs, at this point all you can really do is either accept the facts, push for tougher testing for whatever that's worth, and move on; keep up an imprecise witch hunt that sucks the joy out of the game; or give up on the sport. I vote for the first option.

Besides, while I like to think that if I were a baseball player (extremely large *if* there) confronted with the chance to take steroids in the days before testing, I would have said no . . . I'm not at all sure. In fact, if right now I could take a drug to make myself a better writer, I might very well try it, legal or not. Heck, I've taken illegal drugs that don't remotely enhance performance, and so have millions of other Americans; is it really better because we *weren't* trying to get better at our jobs? I don't want to be an apologist for these players, because they did cheat and then lie over and over again; worst of all in my book, they put a lot of pressure on other players to use steroids just to keep up, which may have health consequences down the road. It's not a good situation. But the way we currently view drugs does not make a lot of sense, and I bet that a few decades from now, we'll be seeing this whole mess from a very different perspective.

It sucks that we can't trust the numbers from an entire era anymore, but on the other hand, think how much fun the stat geeks will have over the next few decades trying to figure out exactly how much of an impact steroids had on individual players and on the game in general. Every era's numbers need to be kept in context anyway, whether because of the dead ball, or segregation, or a higher pitcher's mound, or whatever else—everything already needs to be looked at in context. Now we can just add "or because hundreds of people were injecting cattle hormones into their ass" to the list.

What sucks even more is that we're going to have to relive the whole messy scandal and puffed-up moral outrage every time another player is outed as a user and every time a great but 'roid-tainted player is eligible for the Hall of Fame. We may soon have a Hall that doesn't include the all-time hits leader, single-season home run leader, all-time home run leader, or 354-game winner Roger Clemens, a fairly ridiculous situation.

But hey, maybe it won't seem so crazy years from now, when the next scandal hits, whatever that may be. People my age will sit around in rocking chairs and complain about how much better things used to be back in the good ol' days of pure, innocent HGH.

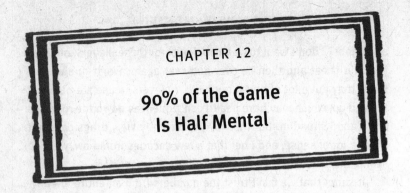

CHAPTER 12

90% of the Game
Is Half Mental

"So, how does this work?" I asked the shrink, my arms crossed in front of me as I lay on the proverbial couch. "Am I supposed to tell you about my childhood, or my dreams, or what?"

He shifted his notebook on his lap, adjusted his glasses, and leaned forward.

"Tell me about Roger Clemens's groin," he said. "Do you think he'll be ready to start on Thursday?"

There's a great line in *Bull Durham* where Crash Davis, the veteran catcher, gives cocky and dim young pitching phenom Nuke LaLoosh a piece of advice: "Don't think. You can only hurt the ball club."

Managers and coaches often talk about a slumping, struggling player by saying that he's trying too hard, or he's pressing, or "he's thinking too much." That always struck me as an amusing and overly positive way of framing a bad situation for the media. A manager can't very well sit there and explain that his player just sucks at the moment, so instead he makes it into a fault of caring too much, putting too much effort in, a flaw that's not really a flaw. Joe Torre was a master of this strategy: "He's pressing a little bit right now. He just needs to stay within himself," he used to say of any and every random hitter on an o-for streak. I never bought it, and both my dad and I used to make fun of it—"Stay within yourself!" was a common nonsense refrain in our house when doing homework, or dishes. The world has a lot of problems, but I don't really think one of them is people thinking *too much*.

Now, though, I wonder if there isn't something to this.

After I got fired from the *Village Voice,* I fell into an especially nasty and long-lasting patch of sleep trouble. I would lie awake for hours and hours, shifting positions futilely, until I could catch an uneasy couple of hours in the very early morning, hardly noticing waking up because it felt like I had never been to sleep. I finally figured there was no point wasting time trying and started simply staying up till four or five or six, reading or watching weird late-night television or surfing the Internet—also wastes of time, I suppose (there are only so many hours that can productively be spent on LOLcats), but not sleeping is less frustrating when you aren't trying so hard. When I noticed the sky turning gray outside my window I'd curse and jump into bed and eventually catch a few hours, once it was too late to do much good. But if I managed to really go under, nothing could wake me—I'd sleep through one, two, or three alarm clocks all blaring at ear-splitting volume, be late to my day job or miss appointments, jerk awake long after the radio alarm had timed itself out, see the time, leap out of bed cursing some more, and maybe frantically call someone or other to apologize. If the Yankees or Mets had a day game, sometimes I woke up after it had already started.

I'm still not really sure if baseball was my problem that summer or my solution. I was clinging to it, but whether it was dragging me down or keeping me afloat was unclear. My idea at the time was to write a book about the 2007 season for both New York teams, as it unfolded, and I decided that meant I would watch every single pitch of every game either team played. (This was made possible by TiVo, the greatest invention of my adult life.) And I did—324 games, more than 1,000 hours of baseball, close to 3,000 innings. That included, just for the home teams, 12,870 plate appearances, 3,199 hits, 308 home runs, 343 stolen bases, and 86 times caught stealing. I watched New York pitchers give up 2,913 hits and 315 home runs, strike out 2,143 opposing batters, and walk 1,148, with 95 wild pitches. When I had an occasional lapse I would watch a couple of innings on fast-forward, but I always made sure I saw everything. I spent more time in the company of the announcers on the YES Network and SNY than with any other human being. And when I wasn't watching baseball I was often reading about it or, if I was being especially social that day, talking about it.

I can't have been a particularly exciting dinner companion that summer. When I tore myself away from the games long enough to meet up with friends, it became apparent that I had absolutely no remaining grasp on current events or culture or, in fact, anything whatsoever besides baseball. Instead of my usual movie a week, I'd only seen two or three all season. I had not been to a concert. I almost never watched anything else on TV because prime-time shows conflicted with the games. I checked the front page of the *New York Times* online once a day or so just to make sure the nuclear apocalypse hadn't started yet, but beyond that I had almost no idea what might be happening in the world, although I read dozens of baseball blogs and my RSS feed was never empty.

"Wait," I would say over dinner with friends, looking around, trying to follow the group's conversation. "Paris Hilton was in jail?" While I wasn't paying attention, astronomers declared that Pluto was not actually a planet.

I was watching baseball for work, and therefore any amount of obsession was justified in my own mind. But no one told me I had to watch every single game both teams played that season—I decided that on my own. What if I missed something? Who was I to pretend I had the authority to write about this if I wasn't completely aware of every single packet of relevant data? Who knew when some offhand comment by an announcer might turn out to be a key to the whole season?

I started out taking notes on every game—who scored how, interesting comments from the announcers, what it all meant for the season. I took my notebook every time I went to Shea or Yankee Stadium and self-consciously wrote in it, angling it away from the fans next to me; I did it at home, too, even though a play-by-play of every game is available online just about instantly. Somewhere around midsummer, however, my notebooks begin to lose focus:

> NOTE TO SELF: Stop using "we." "We need to get another reliever," etc. Not cool. Poor Scott Proctor, though—we DO need to get another reliever. . . .
> Can Pedro come back strong? That would be huge. Biiiig if, though. . . .
> Boston's winning . . . fuck. Fly out—phew. Listless applause. . . .
> Grant Balfour! Yay! Worst pitcher name in baseball! . . .
> Watching Sal Fasano run—oddly mesmerizing. . . .
> What the Christ is that thing on Magglio Ordonez's head? . . .
> Great phrases in the English language: "on deck is Neifi Perez." . . .
> 8/26: Fuuuuck.

Of course, in retrospect it's easy to say that the world would not have ended had I missed a pitch. But I was sure that the one minute I didn't watch would turn out to be the crucial one. And who knows, maybe all that play-by-play detail would have been a useful base of knowledge. We'll never know now, but things might have gone differently if not for the dual misfortunes of Tom Glavine and an (unrelated—at least so far as I can prove) swarm of gnats, on which more later.

The days passed in a fog, differentiated only by the games, the scores, who the Mets were playing, where the Yankees were that day. Get up after noon, walk the dog, read some baseball blogs, surf the Net, walk the dog, maybe do an errand or two, watch both games, walk the dog, stay up till dawn, repeat.

———————

I've had trouble sleeping, off and on, for as long as I can remember. When I was little I thought the evil witch from *Sleeping Beauty* with her creepy glowing green eyes was hiding in my closet, and my dad's nightly pantomime of tossing an imaginary hand grenade in there to blow her up could never fully convince me that she was gone. When I got a little older, I would stay up late reading or, if my parents caught me with the light still on, lying there with my mind racing about whatever it was I had just read.

I'm a night owl by nature anyway; I usually don't start feeling really awake until dinner. When working a nine-to-five job, all too often I end up sleeping from four to seven in the morning, yet somehow that didn't make it any easier to get to sleep the next night. I believe in some cases insomnia is associated with an actual illness, but so far as I know, in my case it was purely psychological, and it's always struck me as an incredibly weird phenomenon. I can't imagine being thirsty, having a pitcher of water right in front of me, and somehow just not drinking it. It forces me to think about, first, how dazzlingly complex the human brain is, and second, how much I hate mine.

I finally went to see a doctor about it a few years back. She advised me to cut back on caffeine—I believe I laughed in her face—and prescribed sleeping pills, Ambien. She said there was a fairly low risk of dependence, and that turned out to be true. What she did not mention, however, were some of the more colorful possible side effects.

I took the Ambien every other night or so for a couple of weeks, though I felt a little uncomfortable with it. But I was getting more sleep than I had been, and if I felt a little out of it the mornings, that was hardly worse than before. Until one night, fifteen or twenty minutes after getting into bed, I started seeing things—dark shapes crawling along the walls and on the ceiling. They were hard to make out exactly, just shadows and silhouettes, but there were long thin limbs, insectlike, and in the corner of my room was a tall figure in a hood. I turned on the bedside lamp, but they didn't go away, which was more than a little disconcerting.

Well, I thought, *either this is an Ambien side effect that no one told me about, or I'm finally going insane.*

In the morning I called the doctor. "Oh, yes," she said, "that can be a side effect. It's fairly uncommon." Good to know. (A few days after that unsettling experience, my friend Julian told me I needn't have been so concerned. "It's *aural* hallucinations that you really have to worry about," he explained. "Seeing things isn't actually all that uncommon. It's when you start hearing voices—that's where the trouble starts." I tossed the Ambien anyway.)

Maybe I should have sought out therapy earlier in life (it's been suggested), but it was the baseball overload in conjunction with the insomnia that finally got me there. It was fall and the playoffs were about to start. I was exhausted enough to finally do something about it, but I didn't want an Ambien repeat, as I was already feeling crazy enough without hallucinations.

The psychiatrist, whom I'll call Dr. B., had his office in a large bare front room of his spacious TriBeCa loft. I was struck by how deliberately empty and sterile the space was, by design, emphasized by all the daylight streaming in through tall windows. It could not have been more different from my own apartment, which is dim, cluttered, covered in dog hair, and the size of Dr. B.'s kitchen island.

I told the doctor a little bit about why I was there, about work and baseball, and that mainly I just wanted to be able to sleep. Then we sat there for a long quiet moment. I wondered if he was already evaluating me, what he might be thinking, how I looked or sounded to him. I asked him what it was I should talk about.

Which is when he mentioned Roger Clemens's groin.

In fact, I was somewhat relieved when the doc turned out to be a Yankees fan, and half our sessions were taken over by baseball talk. I never really gave Dr. B. a fair shot—I didn't feel all that comfortable, didn't want to talk to him about anything personal or embarrassing, and was reluctant to share much about my thought processes once he explained that I really ought to try more "positive thinking." I hate positive thinking.

Furthermore, I felt bad telling him, after several sessions, that I was not feeling any different. I suppose on some level I thought it might hurt his feelings or could seem like a criticism of his therapy skills. While recognizing that telling your therapist everything is fine in order to spare his ego is perhaps a very good sign that you should indeed be in therapy, I always said that things were going a little better.

Now, I'm not a religious person at all, but I do have a tendency to refer to the "baseball gods." I imagine them as a sort of corollary to the Greek gods, the only deities that ever made any kind of emotional sense to me—fallible, emotional, bickering amongst themselves. That, to me, is a far more plausible explanation for the state of the world than one omnipotent being. In any case, if you ever were going to believe in baseball gods, the end of the 2007 New York baseball seasons would have been the time.

As I suspect most people reading this book will vividly recall, the Mets were pretty good that year, despite some sizeable flaws, and spent 158 of their 162 games in first place. Unfortunately, the last day of the season was not one of those 158. Just a short time earlier, the odds of the Mets losing their lead—which had been seven games with seventeen left to play—were minuscule. Baseball Prospectus calculated those odds, in fact, and found the Mets had more than a 90 percent chance of making the playoffs. In the history of the game only a handful of collapses could even come close. Bolstered by these cold, hard facts, I was sure the Mets would pull themselves together and hold off the Phillies; in fact, I had a lot more faith in them than did many of my Mets fan friends, who knew better and were quite bitterly expecting the worst long before there was any logical reason to expect it.

(I cannot prove this at all, but I suspect that if you were to take a poll of New Yorkers, you'd find more insomniac Mets fans than Yankees supporters. Not because the Mets cause insomnia or anything so clear as that. It's just that there is a certain personality type, the kind susceptible to staring at a ceiling crack for hours while exhausted and helpless to keep stray thoughts from flitting all around your skull all night, and I suspect this personality type is slightly more prevalent among Mets fans, that's all.)

Anyway, to make a long and sad story short, future Hall of Famer Tom Glavine started the Mets' final game of 2007, the last Sunday in September, against the Marlins, a team long out of contention—and promptly allowed eight of the nine batters he faced to reach base, including, in the inning's high point, hitting the opposing pitcher with the bases loaded. He allowed seven runs in one solitary third of an inning before being mercifully pulled, but the game was over before it started. The MLB.com write-up of that afternoon included the following phrases: "unfathomable decline," "full-fledged, unconditional meltdown," "spanked by a riled opponent and sent to its room," "desperation to despair," "infamy," and "permanently defaced the resumes of the men who participated in it."

This is when Glavine, who in addition to being one of the best pitchers of his generation and a three-hundred-game winner, was also remarkably adept at handling the media, uncharacteristically compounded his errors by explaining to reporters that this loss was "disappointing" but *not* "devastating," because the latter was a word he reserved for the true tragedies in life. Completely true, but also just about the stupidest thing he could have said at the time.

The Yankees, meanwhile, made the playoffs, but in keeping with their recent habits, they were eliminated in the first round. To be fair, they probably couldn't have gone far anyway, not with their pitching and assorted injuries and lack of well-timed hits, and so it's really misleading to claim that the Yankees lost that year because of a freak swarm of gnats.

Nevertheless: the Yankees lost that year because of a freak swarm of gnats.

I am still not over this. In one of the more flat-out biblical moments I've ever seen on a baseball field, Joba Chamberlain was pitching for the Yankees in Game 2, New York up 1–0, when suddenly a cloud of midges descended on the Indians' ballpark—conveniently located next to a pestilential lake—and covered everything. When I try to explain this to people who aren't baseball fans, they do not believe me. Chamberlain gave up a walk and two wild pitches, which was understandable since he had gnats crawling all over his face and neck, getting into his eyes and mouth. The umpires and players paused the game to spray each other with insect repellant—not something I had previously seen on a baseball field—but it didn't even make a dent.

Later, in the book he cowrote with Tom Verducci, Joe Torre would cite his own failure to pull his team off the field and force a delay here as one of his few regrets. (I can think of a few more he might want to consider, if he's looking for ideas—for example, certain pitching choices in Game 7 of the 2004 ALCS—but nobody asked me.) The Yankees went down 2–0 and had lost the first two games of the best-of-five series. There were a lot of other factors in play there, mainly some uncharacteristically awful pitching from Chien-Ming Wang. (Well, back then it was uncharacteristic.) But it doesn't matter. To me, that will always be the year the Yankees lost because of a swarm of insects. I can only imagine how the baseball gods became *that* pissed off. Perhaps someone in the front office forgot to sacrifice the required white ox.

Just like that, the baseball season ended, and with it went my intense focus of the previous six months. And as it turned out, it was not necessary for me to have watched every minute of every game: it was painfully clear that neither Yankees fans nor, especially, Mets fans were going to be keen to line up to relive the past season. So much for my Subway Series fantasies. I had watched all those pitches in all those innings of all those games for six months, and while I always knew my project would depend on the season's twists and turns, I had never expected such freakishly lousy endings to the local seasons (unusual, for a proud pessimist like myself). I had pinned everything to baseball that summer, time and obsessive focus and fuzzy hopes and dreams. And suddenly it was all over.

Baseball had sucked up most of the hours of my day, but it had also given me some kind of structure, a progression from day to day, something to keep me busy and focused. I still wonder if that fixation was a little dangerous or if it was instead pulling me through. In any case, by the time Dr. B.'s talk had shifted from Roger Clemens's groin to Stephon Marbury's possible bipolar disorder, I was ready to call my therapy quits along with my baseball.

There are many lessons one might choose to take from these events, and from that particular time in my life. I'm still sorting them out. But whatever it all says about me, about the nature of baseball, about the human mind, I am pretty clear on one thing: Tom Glavine owes me money.

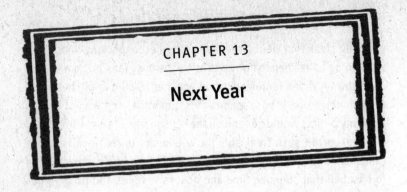

CHAPTER 13

Next Year

Baseball people have been pining for the sport's good old days while complaining about its current problems almost since the game's inception—coaches and fans and writers of almost every era have expressed nostalgic yearning for the previous one. I'd bet that in the third baseball game ever played, spectators and observers were complaining that things had been better back in the first two games, when the sport was still pure.

It's a natural impulse to be drawn to all our warm early memories, or just to an ideal of the good times that we missed out on. Already I sometimes fall into that trap, so I can only imagine how much worse things will get as I age. In a few decades I'll probably be yearning for the magical days of Tony Fernandez, before that whippersnapper Jeter kid took over.

I don't have a lot of patience for these lines of thought. Of course, there are things that are worse about today's game, but there are also plenty of things that are better; the same was true fifty years ago and presumably will still be the case fifty years from now, when the game is played on solar-powered hoverboards and players just implant new body parts instead of bothering with steroids. People don't like change, though, and with the two new ballparks in New York, it's been an especially rough few years for New York fans. Besides that, thanks to the brilliant combination of high prices and a crappy economy, lots of New Yorkers haven't even been able to see much of their new buildings. And these things take some getting used to.

There are a number of legitimate complaints about Citi Field—the name, for one, (soulless and now, as an added bonus, associated with economic collapse and government bailouts) and the faux-quirky irregularity of the right-field dimensions. Lots of ballparks have odd-shaped corners, but it's usually because of something organic in the immediate environment, whereas Citi Field is in the middle of a parking lot and had no need to tailor its dimensions to anything besides the designers' whims. Quirk for its own sake is as cloying in ballparks as it is in indie movies.

Despite a few caveats, Citi Field is in most regards a lovely place. Its best feature is one it shares with the new Yankee Stadium, as the teams partially atone for their avarice: there's now lots of standing room where anyone, regardless of their assigned seat, can watch the game from surprisingly close up. Not everyone is comfortable standing for a long time, but I don't mind it, which means there's no reason I can't buy a $12 seat and then head over to the back of the field-level seats, by first or third base, or out to center field—where there's a bridge with a view at Citi Field, and space on the roof of the restaurant at the new Yankee Stadium—and stake out a prime location. There are better views to be had than I often got at either of the old places. Beyond that, Citi Field boasts generally solid sightlines, nice views of the area (or as nice as is feasible when in Flushing), and a neat idea with the engraved bricks, personalized by fans, that pave the area outside the entrance. It also has excellent food, including the justly famous Shake Shack, and the beer is only overpriced, as opposed to ludicrously overpriced.

And yet I don't think I've heard a single Mets fan express much enthusiasm for the place, even while acknowledging its successes. I think that has more to do with it being strange and unfamiliar, and so completely unlike Shea, than with the park's actual flaws. Some unease is to be expected when you're replacing a building where people have hours and hours' worth of memories and formative experiences. It's going to take years for these new places to feel properly like home, and that would be the case even if their design were flawless.

Citi Field is just not very Mets-like. It's not shaped like Shea, it hardly has Mets colors anywhere, the crowd is arrayed differently. It could almost belong to a brand-new team that had just moved to New York City. As many fans noted as soon as the plans were released, it's more of an homage to the Dodgers, with its Ebbets Field–inspired façade and Jackie Robinson Rotunda, than to the Mets' own history. And though it's never a bad idea to honor Jackie Robinson, the fact is the guy played for the Dodgers and not in Queens, and while Robinson belongs to all of baseball now, it does feel like the Mets are trying awfully hard to claim him. (The Rotunda itself is divided into sections under the labels "Excellence," "Citizenship," "Commitment," "Justice," "Teamwork," "Determination," "Persistence," and "Courage," but it seems to me that the editorializing isn't really necessary.) There aren't many mementos or reminders of previous Mets teams, to the extent that fans howled in protest when the team announced plans to clean Doc Gooden's signature off a wall, where he'd placed it at a fan's request. The team caved, moving the signature instead, and was forced to assure everyone that they would find a way to appropriately honor Mets history.

The fans at Citi Field, at least, seem unchanged. My first game there, the Mets lost to the Marlins 4–3. Johan Santana started and left with the lead, but the bullpen couldn't hold it, leading to the familiar bemoaning I often heard at Shea as the crowd streamed toward the 7 train: "I'm ashamed—no, I am, I'm ashamed," "They spend all that money fixing the bullpen and Johan still gets screwed," "I'm not gonna watch—I'm not even gonna *watch* the Phillies games. It's a fuckin' joke." You can take the Mets fans out of Shea, but you can't take the Shea out of Mets fans, and thank God.

Meanwhile, "put more of an emphasis on team history and tradition" is not something you will ever, ever have to tell the Yankees.

They don't always make it easy to be a fan, the Bombers. I went to the new Stadium for the first time the day after visiting Citi Field, and there had already been months of bad press over very convincing allegations of impropriety in the building's public financing, and weeks of even worse press surrounding the Yankees' stratospheric pricing in the prime field-level seats, resulting in large and embarrassing swaths of empty blue at every home game and uncharacteristically quiet crowds.

I was a little nervous about heading up there for the first time, partly because I'd recently found Citi Field so unfamiliar. I never saw the need for a new Yankee building in the first place, not with so much history at the old place. But I've got to say that while I'm bitter about the new Stadium's prices, outright medieval caste system (the good seats actually have a moat around them), and Hard Rock–ness . . . well, I liked it better than I thought I would. Not that that's saying much.

I was extra-nervous that night because my friend Alex of Bronx Banter, a Yankees blog I contribute to, had gotten me a press pass through the SNY network. So I found myself back in the clubhouse and press box for the first time in a year and a half, my last visit coming at the miserable tail end of the Mets' 2007 season. This time I felt less conspicuous in my ignorance of exactly where to go at what time, since with the new building only open for a couple of weeks, I wasn't alone. It was hard to know which carpeted hallways were closed to the media and which weren't, and so like a sheep I tried to stay close to the herd.

It didn't take too long to settle in this time; it was like riding a bike, if bicycling involved a lot of nudity. I saw several reporters I was happy to see again, and none that I'd been hoping to avoid. I was a little sad to see the dank, dark corridors of the old place replaced. Nothing about the new building was remotely dingy, and though it was a much nicer space, it also felt less behind-the-scenes, less like I was visiting a realm that was off-limits to most people.

It seems unfair to the Yankees' new locker room even to call it a "locker room." It's got to be at least fifteen times bigger than my entire apartment, and the blue neon-backlit frieze at the top, in combination with the personal computer screen at each locker, gives you the impression that the room is about to blast off into space. I felt guilty dragging warning-track dirt onto the plush carpet.

Once again I was reminded of just how much of the job consisted of standing around awkwardly and waiting for people to show up. The most helpful lesson I'd taken with me from my *Village Voice* days was that the notebook was my shield; if I was writing something down, then I had a purpose, could control the narrative, and was able to defuse the awkwardness. So in search of notes to jot down, I wandered around and took in the lockers. Nick Swisher's featured a case of Slump Buster energy drink and, on one side, a collage of all his teammates, with photos clipped from magazines. Other players had photos of their wives or girlfriends, or perhaps just random hot chicks, as the screen savers on their personal monitors. More piles of sneakers, more Tinactin, the occasional bottle of nutritional supplements—all boringly legal.

There were relatively few players around, most of them sticking to the private areas in back, but that was all right, as I had no particularly burning questions to ask this time around. Up close, I actually mistook backup infielder Ramiro Pena for a batboy for several minutes—MLB.com lists him as five-eleven and 165 pounds, but there's no way he's that big, and he looks at most fourteen. I stood in the middle of the floor watching Jorge Posada and Derek Jeter walk back and forth, players I'd been watching closely for more than ten years from one vantage point or another, and though I still didn't feel like I belonged there, I wasn't too uncomfortable, either.

I spent a few minutes in the press box before setting out on a walking tour of the park. Many people have noticed that the crowds at the new place were too quiet, and I'd sensed that from watching on TV, too, but it got properly loud that night, much to my relief, as the Yankees beat the Angels 7–4. Not old Stadium Red Sox loud, or playoff loud, but loud, and when Jeter singled to give the Yankees a lead, it was the same kind of thick, tangible wave of decibels I remember from so many games across the street. There were still plenty of empty $1,250 seats (newly reduced from $2,500), and it hurts to see views like that going to waste, but it didn't seem to make too much of a dent in the cumulative enthusiasm.

My friend Alex had compared it to being inside a pinball machine, and he wasn't wrong: lots of random noises and flashing lights. The featureless blackness of the Mohegan Sun restaurant is unsettling, and the screen in center field is a little overwhelming, very much larger than life, with the players' faces looming like those Easter Island heads. The Great Hall, the huge, imposing outer corridor, complete with massive player flags, that greets fans as they enter is too much—Vegas overkill—and that name sounds like something from Tolkien, one of the scenes you skipped because it was like twelve solid pages of someone singing in Elvish. There are also inexplicably located bars in the place, like Tommy Bahama's and the Jim Beam Suites. Who the hell goes all the way to the Stadium just to sit in a bar with no view of the field and watch the game on TV? Finally, the whole place is so big and so heavily branded that it feels a bit like a theme park: welcome to YankeeWorld™.

I had watched batting practice, though, before I saw most of the place, and it was a reassuring perspective, because from the field the place looks a lot like home. A little lower, a little less steep, a bit more closed-in, but still very Yankee Stadium-ish. There was a lot of continuity in the shape, the colors, the frieze, and it was not as disorienting as I'd feared.

Much of the criticism of the new ballpark has focused, with good reason, on the Yankees' pricing. But the truth is, I haven't been able to afford good seats to a Yankees game since the late nineties. The team screwed over a lot of season-ticket holders with the move to a smaller and pricier park, and I'm angry on their behalf, but I've almost always sat in the upper deck or bleachers anyway, so on a personal level not much has changed. And for all that the team has contorted itself to cater to the superrich, as at Citi Field the bulk of the fans were—for better or worse—the same people I've been seeing at Yankees games my whole life.

I still don't think they needed to build it. And I still hate the way they went about doing it. (I suspect that if I had a better grasp of the complex city budgets and revenue and taxes and everything else involved, I would hate it even more.) But it's here now, and for all its faults, I think I'll be able to enjoy watching a game there. Yes, it's too big, too proud of itself, pompous and over-the-top in places, the embodiment of the unhinged free market. But let's face it: a lot of the time—and I say this with love—so are the Yankees.

The truth is that in the end, I don't think it matters so much what the stadiums are like, at least not to me. How important can any of their problems really be, so long as there's a game on? It *is* infuriating that I can't afford to go to many games at Yankee Stadium, and I'm angry about that, and generally irate about the way the Yankees treat their fans. And yes, once in a while I think I should give up on the sport altogether, that there are better uses for my time and money and energy.

But it's not gonna happen.

On one hand, it's specific details that make the game so great— Keith Hernandez's defense and mustache, El Duque's windup, the view from your usual seats, the ritual of passing the old bat-shaped smokestack outside the old Stadium or the long walk to your gate around Shea's huge circumference.

On the other hand, there will be other details, and what precisely they are isn't so crucial. Some player and stadium idiosyncrasies will be more interesting than the old ones, and some less, but they'll still hold people's attention, still be worth the time.

That's because it's about not just the game, though the game is great, but what it provides for us. Or at least for me. An escape from daily life; numbers and puzzles to figure out; familiar rituals and structure; and people to connect to, parents or friends or total strangers on the subway. You could play baseball with a live halibut instead of a ball and it would still serve the same function, although it would smell worse.

That doesn't mean we shouldn't try to make the game better, or fight to keep ourselves from being priced out, or push for stricter steroid testing, or complain loudly about stadium financing or any of the myriad other legitimate problems facing the game. But it does mean that I don't have a whole lot to threaten the powers that be with, because however worked up I might get, I just don't see myself giving it up. It's alarming to consider just how many major felonies it might take for me to even consider walking away.

Recently I've been having a lot of odd, vivid baseball dreams, the kind it takes you a couple of minutes to shake off once you're awake. There was one where Derek Jeter and Alex Rodriguez had been kidnapped, and for some reason the police were no help, and it was up to me to rescue them, racing against the clock. In another I showed up in class only to discover everyone taking a final exam I had no idea was coming, and all the questions were about the '94 strike, and I couldn't answer any of them. The most memorable one happened just a few weeks ago, and had me inexplicably making out with Johan Santana at an Enrique Iglesias concert. The subconscious is a funny place, but I guess it makes sense for baseball to crop up all over mine.

I still watch games with more detachment than I used to, though probably not with any more cynicism than the average fan these days, and not with any less enjoyment than I used to. It's still the best soap opera on television, and something I look forward to distracting myself with after a bad day or rewarding myself with after a good day. As of this writing, I have no clear idea of what I'll do next, of where I'll end up working, or if I'll ever set foot in a locker room again. There are an awful lot of unknowns. But one thing I'm sure of is that wherever I find myself and whatever else I'm doing, I'll still be watching. Maybe that's worth something all by itself.

ACKNOWLEDGMENTS

This book wouldn't have been possible without the help of many, many people, but please don't hold that against them.

My editors, Becca Shapiro and Jill Schwartzman, were remarkably kind and patient, and stuck with me the whole way . . . plus, they were pretty much always right. It was almost annoying. Note to Yankees fans: The next time you see Becca at the Stadium in her Brian Roberts Orioles jersey, *please do not spit on her,* regardless of the final score. Thank you.

I was extremely lucky to meet my agent Chris Parris-Lamb close to the start of his career, because now he's really too successful to be putting up with the likes of me. Nevertheless, he does, and he had my back throughout.

While this book couldn't have happened without a lot of people, it *especially* couldn't have happened without Dave Blum, who really took a chance on me—my firstborn child is his if he wants it. Megathanks, too, to Alex Belth of Bronx Banter, who helped me get started blogging years ago, and has helped me with a lot more since.

Thanks to Junwei Yu, for showing me around in Taiwan and teaching me a ton about baseball there; and to Linda, the blood-donating Mets fan, for letting me write about her.

Without my friends I would have gone insane, or at least a lot more insane, pretty early on in this process. That's especially true of Katharine Critchlow, who tolerated hours of the YES Network and went with me to sports bars of varying repute, fed me, got me out of the apartment, watched both *Troll* and *Troll 2* with me, and was generally awesome. So were a number of other people, but particularly Tom O'Donnell, Ted Rounsaville, Julian Graham, Katie Aldrich, and Mara Altman—so thanks, guys.

Finally, my parents, Jon Katz and Paula Span. I have my dad to thank for getting me involved in baseball to begin with, of course, and for his many life lessons—such as "follow your bliss," and "The world is full of peckerheads, toothless ducks, and midgets. Don't let them get you down."

I don't mention my mom as often in this book, just because she's not much of a baseball fan. But she is a great writer and editor, full of good advice, and supportive at a level far above and beyond genetic obligation. Also, because she was worried that she would come off as kind of stolid and uninteresting based on my brief description of her, I hasten to add that in a number of ways she's actually quite odd.

I'd like to close by thanking Mariano Rivera. Not because he helped with the book or anything . . . just for existing.

EMMA SPAN has written about baseball for the *Village Voice,* *Slate,* the *New York Press,* and popular blogs such as Bronx Banter, among many other publications; yet when she appeared on *Jeopardy!* in the fall of 2009, she missed an easy question about Mickey Mantle (claiming that "the buzzer timing was really tricky"). She graduated from Yale University in 2003 and now lives in Brooklyn. This is her first book.